Evaluating Management Development, Training and Education

To:

Anna, Sam, Sarah and Sophie

Evaluating Management Development, Training and Education

Second edition

Mark Easterby-Smith

Gower

First edition published 1986 by
Gower Publishing Co Ltd as
Evaluation of Management Education, Training and Development

Second edition published by
Gower Publishing
Gower House
Croft Road
Aldershot
Hampshire GU11 3HR
England

Gower
Old Post Road
Brookfield
Vermont 05036
USA

British Library Cataloguing in Publication Data

Easterby-Smith, Mark
  Evaluating Management Development,
  Training and Education – 2 Rev.ed
  I. Title
  658.407124   *Po 4386*

    ISBN 0–566–07307–2

Library of Congress Cataloging-in-Publication Data

Easterby-Smith, Mark
    Evaluating management development, training and education – Mark Easterby-Smith—2nd ed.
        p. cm.
    Rev. ed. of: Evaluation of management education, training and development. c1986
    Includes bibliographical references and index.
    ISBN 0–566–07307–2; $58.95 (approx.)
    1. Management—Study and teaching—Evaluation.   I. Easterby-Smith, Mark. Evaluation of management education, training and development.   II. Title.
  HD30.4.E26 1993
  658.4'0712404—dc20   93–1818
                                                                              CIP

Phototypeset in Palatino by Intype, London and
printed in Great Britain at the University Press, Cambridge.

Contents

List of figures

Preface

Much water has passed under the bridge since the first edition of this book appeared in 1986. The world has seen several wars, the dismantling of the Soviet Union and the establishment of a new balance of power; the boom years of the mid to late 1980s have been replaced by a deep recession led, if that is the right word, by the USA; and in the UK the aggressive free market ideas of Margaret Thatcher have been replaced by the more conciliatory social awareness of John Major.

In the more parochial world of evaluation there have been some developments, although none has been truly revolutionary. Several new books have appeared which cover the evaluation of training in general, without paying undue attention to the special problems of evaluating *management* training or to the increasingly important area of management education. Recent works such as Phillips (1987), Bramley (1991) and Newby (1992) still draw heavily on 'traditional' approaches to evaluation. Thus they concentrate on the technical aspects of evaluation rather than the political elements, they retain the 'systematic' model of training as the starting point of their prescriptions, and they pay scant attention to the enormous changes that have taken place in the practice of management learning during the last few years. These changes include the fact that in Europe management and business qualifications have become firmly established, both in higher education and in corporate career structures, leading to closer collaboration between the two sectors. And in the UK, as a result of the Constable and Handy reports of 1987 and the subsequent Management Charter Initiative (MCI), management education has come to occupy a high place on the business agenda.

The first edition of this book was born out of frustration on two counts. First, that after an initial flowering of literature around 1970 (such as Hesseling, 1966; Warr, Bird and Rackham, 1970; Hamblin, 1974), very little on the evaluation of training was published in the following years; indeed most of the original books were allowed to go out of print. Second, in the same period, considerable developments in evaluation theory and practice in educational and programme evaluation did not seem to enter the mainstream of training literature, such as it was. I came to realize that there was very little that could be recommended to students and managers working in this area and that there was a need for a new book to provide an overview, while also making available to the management training community some of the newer ideas on evaluation which had emerged in related fields, especially in the USA. The resulting *Evaluation of Management Education, Training and Development* was published in 1986.

This second edition continues in the spirit of the first, by providing a further updating of ideas and developments in related fields, where evaluation methods have continued to evolve. I have also included new studies, many based on those I have conducted in companies and educational establishments since the publication of the first edition, or on work conducted by other colleagues. In addition I have given more space to developments and practices outside the UK, particularly in continental Europe, to reflect the increasing globalization of business and the growing integration of management and education.

As before, the book covers a range of educational, training and developmental interventions in the management field. It aims to continue to question, and provide a critique of, the 'established' methods of evaluation, while adding insights and examples from leading evaluation practice both in the UK and overseas.

Mark Easterby-Smith

PART I

Aims and purposes

1 Introduction

The last decade has been paradoxical for management education and development. When the economies of most Western countries were faltering in the early 1980s there were severe cuts both in corporate training and in higher education. During the 'boom' years of the mid-1980s there was some stability in both areas, although the widespread philosophy of privatization meant that many company trainers were being hived off to work independently, but under contract to their original employers. Now, in the early 1990s, industrialized countries are in the grip of another severe recession and a tough retrenchment could be reasonably expected throughout the training world. But this is not the case so far: many leading companies are asserting their belief in training as the key to future competitiveness, and governments have encouraged an era of rapid expansion in higher education.

During this time views about the significance and contribution of evaluation have changed too. During the early 1980s evaluation was linked to demonstrating the value of the training function in order to justify its own continued existence to top managers, funders, and other decision makers; in the mid-1980s there was more interest in developing and standardizing evaluation procedures in order to maintain and develop what was already there; and in the early 1990s, where the growth in provision is leading to greater internal competition, the emphasis is on different providers demonstrating the quality of their products.

These are broad generalizations, of course. There is much variation below the surface in terms of local practices, problems and purposes. For a whole range of reasons – cultural, historical, economic and structural – developments in evaluation techniques have differed in other countries when compared with the UK. My aim, therefore, in this second edition is to refine and update some of the ideas and models developed in the earlier edition in the light of social and economic changes that have taken place since the mid-1980s, while broadening examples of application to other contexts in the UK and abroad.

The starting point, as before, is that evaluation is a complex process which cannot easily be divorced from issues of power, politics, value judgements and human interests. An emphasis on the pure technicalities of questionnaire design, data collection and presentation may give the impression of scientific impartiality, but it is illusory. Choices about ways of gathering data and the design of evaluation procedures should be made with some knowledge of the range of methods available and, most importantly, with some understanding of the uses to which the evaluation may be put. It is depressing to see how often trainers and their institutions design end-of-course questionnaires (sometimes known as 'happiness sheets'), in compliance with some notion of good training practice, without any clear view of the purpose that the exercise is intended to serve. It is this question that will be considered in some depth in the next chapter of the book.

Having recognized the complexities inherent in evaluation, I have attempted to provide the reader with guidance to some of the difficult decisions that need to be made, and illustrations of how they can work in practice. There are no easy prescriptions for success, and this book does not pretend to provide such. Nevertheless, there are many simple ideas contained herein, which people might like to use in their own work, provided that they are willing to reject firmly those approaches which do not seem to be bearing any fruit.

With regard to the evaluation of training there are a number of authors who have been particularly influential over the last three decades. A series of articles by Donald Kirkpatrick in the *Journal of the American Society for Training and Development* is still regarded by many as the classic guidance on evaluation, although others would argue that the problems of training have moved on a long way since that series was first published (Kirkpatrick, 1959/60). In Holland, Peter Hesseling (1966) published a significant book which stressed the importance of making explicit to trainees the purpose of any evaluation study; and Warr, Bird and Rackham (1970) and Tony Hamblin (1974) made useful contributions in the UK, primarily by combining some of Kirkpatrick's ideas with a concern for the objectives of a training event. Since then there has been little of significance in the UK other than the first edition of this book (1986), and a recent book by Peter Bramley (1991). The latter, although it acknowledges some of the different styles towards evaluation that might be adopted, still concentrates on the technicalities.

I shall return to each of these five works at different stages in this book; but for now it seems important to indicate four main ways in which this book is distinctive from the mainstream of evaluation work in the training world.

First, although these authors claim to cover the evaluation of management training, their models and examples feature courses for supervisors; such courses have, in theory at least, straightforward goals and objectives. In contrast, this book is concerned with the evaluation of training and development of managers who are essentially working in roles that cannot be codified and where training objectives are much more problematic. I shall be returning later in this chapter to the question of what is meant by management.

The second important difference is that these earlier works concentrate on the evaluation of courses. The early 1970s represented the heyday of management and supervisory courses, and approaches to the training and development of managers have evolved significantly during the last decade. Ideas such as action learning, self-development, and work-related learning have become essential weapons in the armoury of people involved in management training and development. There has been a consequent reduction in the popularity of formal courses and workshops, and much attention has been given to getting line managers to take direct responsibility for management development – often with the background help of the original trainees. This blurring of the boundaries between 'learning' and 'working' makes sense to those who are concerned about the failure of formal courses to have much impact upon behaviour on the job; but it poses obvious difficulties for evaluators who might be interested in establishing whether, for example, these new approaches to management development have any more impact than conventional ones.

The third difference is that those other authors, although providing simple frameworks for looking at evaluation, have concentrated on the different *measurement techniques* that can be applied in different situations. Recent developments in evaluation, while not denying the value of measurement, have tended to place rather greater emphasis upon the question of how the information will actually be used, on the practicalities of implementation, and on the ethics of evaluation practice. And this is certainly borne out by my own experiences which show that increasing sophistication of measurement techniques is of no avail within evaluation if basic questions about purposes, roles, and implementation have not already been considered.

Finally, there is a strong flavour of 'systems thinking' in the earlier books. By that I mean an emphasis on the measurement of outputs from a given process (i.e. a course) which is then fed back to those responsible for providing the inputs to the process so that they can assess whether those inputs (i.e. lectures) are appropriate, and whether they need to be changed. Although the systems model is often of considerable use in evaluation work, it is not the only approach to evaluation, and there are occasions when other approaches are con-

siderably more appropriate. Again, some of these alternative approaches will be considered in this book, particularly in Chapter 2.
In view of all this, I have four main aims in writing this book:

1   To update the field of evaluation so that it will be more able to deal with the newer approaches to the development of managers that have been adopted in the last fifteen years or so.
2   To incorporate some of the ideas that have evolved in the evaluation of social and general educational programmes, particularly within the USA, into the practice of *management* education and training evaluation.
3   To make explicit some of the choices that are available for those involved in evaluation, and to provide some guidance to those involved in making these choices.
4   To illustrate the choices and issues that can be encountered in conducting real evaluations in a wide range of contexts.

What is management?

Having stressed that this book emphasizes the evaluation of *management* training and development, it will be necessary to clarify these terms before embarking on the main discussion. If we start with the term 'management' there is a fairly straightforward distinction to make between management as a class of people, and management as an activity. 'Management' people are those who carry the title of manager and who commonly share similar beliefs about their status, the right to manage, and so on. Conventionally the title of manager is given to people who are one or more levels above the supervision of operatives in the organizational hierarchy. This definition can be applied most easily in the traditional manufacturing organization. Unfortunately the decline of the manufacturing sector in Western economies, the development of non-hierarchical organizational structures, and the increasing importance of specialist and professional roles within organizations mean that this way of defining a manager is becoming increasingly inapplicable.

Both the title of 'manager' and the links to organizational hierarchy are products largely of Anglo-Saxon culture. Curiously enough, although the word 'manage' has French origins (either *maneger* which means to school horses, or *ménager* which means to organize a household), the French rarely use the term 'manager' and prefer *cadre*. Within the French system *cadres* are defined as such by their initial education within the highly elitist *grandes écoles*. This is largely dependent on their social class, and has little to do with performance or position in the organizational hierarchy. A similar point can be made about Germany where there is no linguistic equivalent for 'manager'; instead, German organizations are run primarily by highly respected engineers (Lawrence 1992).

Another attempt to define a manager is by recognition of the symbols of their status, by the clothes they wear or the cars they drive. But this has obvious problems if one is trying to understand management within different countries, and there is one more problem: even if these were accurate indicators of *who* is a manager they tell us virtually nothing about *what* he or she does.

Perhaps, therefore, it is more helpful to consider the activity of 'managing', whether or not it is being undertaken by people who hold the formal labels of managers. Those people who have studied the activity of managing in the past may be grouped into a number of 'schools'. I shall briefly summarize some of the main ideas of managing from four of these schools, since views of 'management' can greatly influence approaches taken towards the development of managers, and consequently the evaluation of whatever procedures are established to achieve this.

The classical school

This has for most of this century been the conventional wisdom about management. It states what managers do – or at least, what they *should* do if they are to be considered as real managers. One of the well-known acronyms for the task of a manager is POSDCORB. These letters stand respectively for the activities of planning, organizing, staffing, directing, co-ordinating, reporting, and budgeting. These ideas all seem to have their origins in the personal experiences of a few men (Fayol, 1916; Gulick, 1937). They have been enormously influential to the extent that whenever practising managers are asked what it is that managers do, they start talking about planning, organizing, and so on. Moreover, the 'principles of management' are still reproduced, largely uncritically, every year on many management courses around the world. But, as Mintzberg (1973) points out in his classic study, it is almost impossible to identify these principles of management in operation when managers are either observed or questioned in depth about their behaviour, regardless of whether or not they are judged to be effective managers.

The decision theory school

Of rather more recent origin (Simon, 1959) is the view that the primary activity of a manager – and what distinguishes a good manager from a bad manager – is the ability to make the right decision in conditions of uncertainty. This school of thought has emerged from economics, but is distinguished by acceptance that decision making is not necessarily a 'rational' process – which has also led to the widely accepted view that managers should attempt to make decisions which will work (satisficing) within given constraints, rather than searching for the best possible decision that could be made in any circumstances (optimizing) (Cyert and March, 1963). This particular approach has led to an emphasis within management education and consultancy upon providing tools to help managers make the essential decisions that they presumably need to make in their jobs. 'Management Science' and 'Operational Research' are two academic disciplines which have grown up around the assumed importance of decision making. Indeed, decision making may sometimes be an important feature of a manager's job (whether or not the decisions are amenable to the quantitative techniques devised by management scientists), and the growing emphasis on satisficing rather than optimising suggests that the practical outcomes of decisions are rather more important than the sophistication of techniques that go into making them. And so it is quite easy to question whether decision making is *all* there is, or should be, to the manager's job.

The work activity school

Henry Mintzberg took the trouble to spend a few weeks observing closely what a small number of senior managers actually *did* with their time. His observations (Mintzberg, 1973) conflicted very much with the conventional view of a manager planning and directing the enterprise in a detached way. The activity of real managers appeared to be characterised by brevity, variety, and fragmentation: managers did an enormous number of different things in a day, most of them lasted for very short periods of time, and the manager's concentration was continually being interrupted by other pressures. The individuals Mintzberg observed tended to have a preference for 'live action': they would telephone people rather than write memoranda to them, and this meant an enormous amount of time talking to people in meetings, both scheduled and unscheduled. Whether, of course, managers *should* behave in this way is a moot point. Although it would seem from Mintzberg's studies that most of these features of managerial work are unavoidable, and the question should therefore be about how managers can best be helped to deal with all the complexities and diversity in their jobs.

Competence and postmodernism

The last few years have seen the emergence of two distinct lines of thought about management, 'competence' and 'postmodernism'. These, in some ways, are in opposition to each other.

In the UK there has been much interest in the idea of 'managerial competence' – that it is possible to specify a list of traits and behaviours which will be possessed by an effective manager, and that to some extent they are transferable. This underlies moves by the National Council for Vocational Qualifications (NCVQ) to establish standards for all levels of management training in the UK. Although a great deal of work has been funded recently from government sources in order to define levels of competence, much of it is based on older pieces of work. These include Mintzberg's list of eight basic skills (Mintzberg, 1973), Burgoyne and Stuart's list of eleven managerial skills (Burgoyne and Stuart, 1976) and the identification by Boyatsis of twenty-one managerial competences (Boyatsis, 1982). However, these recent moves to codify and standardize competencies have also attracted their share of criticism, on the grounds that competences must vary significantly from context to context, that the attempt to standardize may lead to unnecessary emphasis on those aspects that are measurable, and that the technical exercise of producing lists of competences sidesteps moral and ethical dilemmas associated with the professionalization of management (Burgoyne, 1989).

In contrast, although not yet in conscious opposition, to the view of a standardized competences is a collection of ideas, developed largely by French philosophers, known as postmodernism. This is mainly an attack on 'modernism' – the view that progress in the world can best be achieved by the application of scientific methods and rational problem-solving. Postmodernism posits a rejection of rational and objective methods for solving social and organizational problems (Carter and Jackson, 1990). It takes many forms and has numerous expressions. In architecture, for example, it involves a rejection of large rectangular, 'efficient' buildings in favour of smaller, more complex and varied buildings. The inclusion of classic arches, pyramids, jagged outlines and varied colours reinforces the rejection of standardized forms, and shows a willingness to derive ideas from any source. In sociology it takes the form of a critique of the power of the modern state and of the control that society exercises over individuals, often through highly subtle linguistic means such as distinguishing between 'normal' and 'abnormal' behaviour (Sturrock, 1979).

The implications for management include, therefore, a critique of the rationalistic and analytic approaches that have formed the basis of conventional Master of Business Administration (MBA) programmes, and a questioning of the goals that managers are apparently serving. It may be asked to what extent are managers the willing or unwilling servants of social control as the corporate states represented by multi-nationals become increasingly powerful? In whose interests are the current forms of progress, and should there be an ethical base to managerial action? Above all, the postmodern perspective questions both the purpose and certainty embodied in views of modern management. Management is best seen as an eclectic activity with many principles and methods but no clear way of deciding which are best.

Summary

Not surprisingly, there is little consensus among academics about the nature of management and managerial work. Although it is clearly not the final solution, a useful summary of key features of managerial work was produced by Burgoyne, Boydell and Pedler (1978), based on an overview of the literature, particularly from the 'work activity' school. Four inter-related features were identified as follows:

1   Managerial work is complex and variable.
2   Managers exist in order to deal with unprogrammed, as opposed to programmed, problems.
3   Managerial work involves ordering and co-ordinating the work of others, but to do this managers must first be able to create similar order and co-ordination in themselves.
4   Managers need to be able to move and work across technical, cultural, and functional boundaries, and this demands an ability to adapt quickly and to have 'learned how to learn'.

The role of training, development and education of managers

It should be clear from the above discussion that there is no general agreement about what managers do, nor about what they should do. And there is yet further diversity when one considers the activity of managing, from at least two more sources.

First, there may be differences in managerial activity according to the type and context of the organization in which the manager is working. It takes little imagination to realize that the manager in a steel rolling mill will spend his or her time in a substantially different way from a counterpart who is managing a research laboratory or a branch of an insurance company; similarly a McDonalds outlet in Zambia is likely to pose very different managerial problems to an outlet in the USA.

Second, as Rosemary Stewart has demonstrated (Stewart, 1976, 1982), there is a substantial amount of choice available to any manager about how to do the job. And it is quite common to find two managers with almost identical jobs in the same organization tackling those jobs in very different ways.

Given this diversity of managerial activity it is not surprising that a very wide range of approaches have evolved which are aimed at making managers more effective in whatever jobs they have undertaken. I have chosen to use the terms, training, development, and education in this book simply because they are widely used in relation to managerial learning. They do not fully cover all the procedures that are available, nor can the three terms be distinguished precisely from each other in many practical instances, but they provide a useful starting point. I do not find helpful the traditional distinction between training and development: that training is aimed at improving managers' current performance, and development is aimed at improving managers' future performance. Not only does the distinction sound too good to be true, but it also seems dubious to base definitions upon the apparent goals of programmes when, as we shall see in Chapter 1, the whole notion of goals and objectives is extremely problematic.

My preference is to view *training* as a procedure involving managers attending, at least in part, courses or workshops – which still may vary in process from highly structured instruction to self-directed approaches such as learning communities (Meggison and Pedler, 1975). Training may also take place on the job without the framework of any course structure. For example, I would include within this rather broad definition of training such procedures as coaching by the boss, study assignments, and many of the activities involved within 'action learning'.

It is, however, in the area of on-the-job training that the distinction between this and *development* becomes rather blurred. It can be argued that training should be seen merely as a sub-system of management development (Ashton and Easterby-Smith, 1978), but for the present it will suffice to think of developmental procedures within organizations as being things like appraisals, potential assessments, career development schemes, job rotation, and so on. Also, in using the term development here I am concerned only with the procedures that may be established, and not with the potential outcomes from them – which often may be described as learning or development for the managers involved.

One of the aspects of management development that has received increasing attention in recent years, has been that of self-development. Whereas there normally tends to be an emphasis within training and development on making the procedure of some relevance to the manager's job, self-development can in theory take place quite independently of any work-related considerations. This characteristic is shared with *management education* – which is, of course, the point at which the distinction between development and education becomes blurred. Most management education is conducted within the walls of universities, colleges, *grandes écoles* and other educational institutions. The awards of degrees, diplomas, and other certificates of educational attainment, according to different schools of thought, indicate either that the individual already has most of the knowledge and skills required for successful performance as a manager, or that he or she has demonstrated some interest in adopting a managerial career and might therefore be considered to have some management potential.

As I have indicated above, in some countries formal management education forms the essential route of access to highly paid jobs in industry, and it can also provide an opportunity for people to switch careers from less to more prestigious sectors of employment (Whitley, Thomas and Marceau, 1981).

Many major companies have funded management education centres for a number of years. Here managers attend short courses which do not lead to any form of accreditation other than having their 'cards marked'. However, the rise in managerial qualifications, especially MBAs, has led to increased interest in linking internal training to some kind of external accreditation. This is now being provided independently by universities through the establishment of in-company MBAs, or by national accreditation councils such as NCVQ and the MCI which enable attendance at short courses to accumulate into credits which can be converted into nationally recognized qualifications. In consequence, many companies are starting to work much more closely with educational institutions and short courses are starting to reflect some of the requirements of formal education as well as practical elements of technical and skill training.

Thus the traditional distinction between training, education and development may be becoming increasingly blurred. And other trends over the last few years which include shorter, more specific, courses, more attempts to integrate training with normal work, and increasing emphasis being placed on the line manager's (rather than the training specialist's) responsibilities suggest that this blurring will continue. It is partly because of the difficulty in differentiating between these terms that this book covers the evaluation of all three.

There is, however, a more important point. As has been stated above, one of the main reasons for writing the book is to indicate that evaluation is not simply a matter of dishing out the odd questionnaire at the end of courses, but that there are many other considerations to be taken into account if such questionnaires are to be of any use. In my experience many of the problems that occur in evaluation are to be found in the contexts of all three procedures, and therefore a book which examines evaluation of management training, development, *and* education is likely to throw rather more light on each of them.

A number of these problems will be considered in this part of the book, beginning in Chapter 1 with the critical issues of the *purpose* of evaluation. And they will be encountered more extensively in Part III which considers examples of practical applications of evaluation in a range of circumstances.

2 Purposes and styles of evaluation

Strictly speaking, training programmes and management development procedures do not have purposes in their own right. It is only people who have purposes. Similarly, there are many reasons why people may wish to conduct evaluations of procedures. For example, they may be wishing to: document events, record student changes, identify points of institutional vitality, place the blame for trouble on others, aid administrative decision making, facilitate corrective action, increase understanding of teaching and learning processes, make a case for greater resources, and so on. It is only in an indirect sense that evaluations may be seen to contain any purposes of their own since their designs may embody the purposes of their instigators.

The purposes of individuals may cover such a wide range of aims that it is not feasible to provide an adequate framework for analysis (though we shall encounter a number of apparent individual purposes later in this book, in the case studies); but it is possible to talk in more general terms about the purposes of evaluation studies. This will therefore form a starting point to this chapter, and it is also suggested that it should form a starting point to any evaluative activity. There are several reasons for this.

First, there is some logic to the idea of being clear about why one is jumping into an activity before one does it – and a great deal of what passes for evaluation fulfils little more than a ritualistic function; the end-of-course questionnaire is circulated at the end of the course simply because people expect it to be there.

Second, although some would disagree with this point, it is likely that a confusion over the purposes of an evaluation study will make it less able to serve adequately any single one of those purposes.

Third, one of the difficulties in effecting implementation of evaluation work is that many of those involved tend to be rather circumspect about their true interests and purposes. It is, therefore, likely that some concentration upon identifying the purpose of an evaluation may help to flush out some of the hidden agendas of those involved. Not that this will solve all the problems of the evaluator; but it might provide a reasonable start.

Four general purposes of evaluation

Although, as we shall see later, the approaches and styles towards evaluation adopted by authors and practitioners are almost as varied as their proponents, there is quite a high degree of consistency about what they consider to be the primary aim underlying their evaluative activities. The four discussed here are: *proving, improving, learning* and *controlling*. The first aims to demonstrate conclusively that something has happened as a result of training or developmental activities, and that this may also be linked to judgements about the value of the activity: whether the right thing was done, whether it was well done, whether it was worth the cost, and so on. The second aim, 'improving', implies an emphasis on trying to ensure that either the current, or future programmes and activities become better than they are at present. The third aim recognizes that evaluation cannot with ease be divorced from the processes upon which it concentrates, and therefore that this slight problem might well be turned to advantage by regarding evaluation as an integral part of the learning and development process itself. The fourth aim, controlling, is a very common activity for evaluation and involves using evaluation data to ensure that individual trainers are performing to standard, or that subsidiary training establishments are meeting targets according to some centrally determined plan. These four general purposes are illustrated in Figure 2.1 – where I have added a label to the gap in the centre of the four overlapping circles: this is the *ritual* function performed by evaluation questionnaires at the end of courses.

The emphasis on these four aims has changed over the years. The first three aims roughly parallel historical developments in evaluation thought during the 1960s, 1970s, and early 1980s; the fourth has assumed growing importance in recent years as large organizations in both the public and private sectors have invested heavily in management training but have diversified, or contracted out, its provision. The increasing competition between institutions has meant that training and educational establishments have become increasingly concerned to monitor and control the performance of individual teachers. Inevitably there are overlaps; but although authors generally acknowledge the

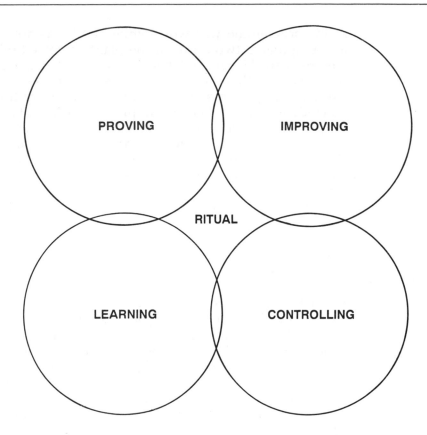

Figure 2.1 Four general purposes of evaluation

possibility of different purposes, they usually display a preference for one only. Moreover, there are also reasons why an evaluator may choose one particular aim over the others, beyond the dictates of fashion and methodological development. It would seem that economic pressures are placing an increasing onus upon the evaluator to prove the worth of training and other developmental activities. But before discussing the issue of choice it seems worth elaborating a little on the background to each of these general aims.

Proving

The emphasis on proving the worth and impact of training began in the USA. There, the first major evaluation study was that conducted during the Second World War, when the Training Within Industry (TWI) organization ran courses lasting ten hours through which over one million American supervisors received training. When asked by the House Appropriations' Committee for evidence that the expenditure on this programme was worthwhile, TWI was able to provide figures indicating that in two-thirds of the plants involved production increases of more than 25 per cent had been recorded since the training had taken place. Although it is probable that these production increases were caused by factors other than the supervisory training programme, this evidence was sufficiently impressive to maintain TWI in existence – and it was even exported to Europe after the war as part of the attempt to reconstruct national industries (Hesseling, 1966, pp. 45–7).

While the results in the TWI provided adequate evidence according to the standards of the time, it is unlikely that this would be given much credence by modern researchers. Indeed, as standards of acceptability have risen, successful cost-benefit evaluations have been reported most infrequently. In the case of operative training there are a number of cases where evaluation studies have been able to make modest estimates of the financial benefits resulting from highly specified forms of training (Jones and Moxham, 1969; Gibb, 1972). But, as Hamblin (1974) points out, the problems become exceedingly difficult when considering the discretionary and non-programmable aspects of managerial work. Even in the present day there remain few convincing cost-benefit evaluations of management training, and opinion remains divided upon whether it is worth attempting. For example, a report to the Manpower Services Commission on the costing of training by Peat, Marwick, Mitchell and Company commented that although cost-benefit analysis might be appropriate for considering the economic and social effects of public investments in training and education on a 'grand' scale, 'the method does not seem appropriate for judging investments in training by an individual company' (Peat, Marwick, Mitchell and Company, 1979). Nevertheless, cost-benefit analysis of management training is still recommended by some authors (Salinger and Deming, 1982, p. 26), as the 'ultimate assessment'. Unfortunately, the example given by these authors is of a study which did not go beyond analysis of the potential cost-benefits of a programme, which was never run. To their credit they were able to demonstrate that the programme should *not* be run because the maximum potential benefits were likely to be far less than the costs of the programme. But the approach of cost-benefit analysis does not present the most optimistic future for evaluation.

Nevertheless, it has been argued by influential authorities such as Michael Scriven (1967), that evaluators should always attempt to examine the *value* of any particular programme. According to Hesseling (1966, p. 44), 'evaluation research aims at providing a systematic and comprehensive measure of success or failure for training programmes'. But, the problem remains that even if it is possible to overcome the technical difficulties in measuring outcomes and changes resulting from managerial training and development, it has still to be decided against whose criteria of value such changes might be assessed. As Hopwood has pointed out in an interesting discussion on the meaning of corporate effectiveness, notions of what are good and desirable behaviours for managers are not universal. They may be presented as if they are self-evident and objectively determined, but in fact they are often articulated primarily to serve the interests and demands of powerful groups within organizations, 'and as such interests and contexts vary and change over time, so do the prevailing notions of effectiveness' (Hopwood, 1979, p. 82). So, also, it is with notions of the value of procedures intended to change managerial behaviour.

Before leaving this discussion about the problems of *proving* the effects of management training it is worth noting two possible ways of resolving the problem of having multiple criteria of value.

First, those involved in evaluation might identify the most influential stakeholders in relation to the programme and simply attempt to present evaluative information within the framework of value held by each individual. (The notion of a stakeholder has been expanded in recent years as an acknowledgement that people other than investors – such as employees and members of the community in which the organization is situated – may have a legitimate interest in an organization. The notion of 'stakeholder' may be employed in a similar way towards management training and developmental activities, and therefore could include 'learners' or trainees, their bosses, colleagues, families, subordinates, and so on.)

Second, one might take a more catholic approach by identifying all the main stakeholders involved with the programme, and attempting to identify what criteria they would use in assessing the value of the programme. Peter Critton (1982) recommends this approach in relation to clients, learners, designer/change agents, and the organization. Any evaluative information can then be collected with these multiple criteria in mind.

Improving

Michael Scriven (1967) placed emphasis on assessing the *value* of a programme (a summative role); this was formulated in contrast to an earlier view of Cronbach (1963, p. 236) that 'the greatest service evaluation can perform is to identify aspects of the course where revision is desirable'. This he labelled as *formative* evaluation which is aimed at *improving* whatever product is under investigation. Writers on the evaluation of management training have tended to stress this particular purpose, partly as a reaction to the difficulties of *proving* anything about the effects of training. Thus, Warr, Bird and Rackham (1970, p. 18) state that 'the primary purpose of gathering evaluation and data is to provide the trainer with information which will help him increase his subsequent effectiveness'. And Hamblin (1974, p. 72), after some hopeful comments earlier in the book about the analysis of potential benefits, comments that the purpose of evaluation 'is not to determine if desired changes did occur but rather to *determine what should happen next . . .'*

There is vast support for *improving* as a valid purpose to evaluation, although one suspects that but for technical difficulties many authors would have preferred this to have been a purpose subsidiary to *proving*. Nevertheless, in a more positive sense there has been a considerable amount of work conducted recently which views evaluation as an aid to decision making. Some of this will be discussed later in the chapter.

Learning

The possibility that evaluation may contribute directly to the *learning* process has received less attention in the literature than either of the above two purposes. But there are still one or two examples. Warr, Bird, and Rackham (1970), provide evidence of a pre-course questionnaire, administered as part of an evaluation study, having a positive impact on the learning of supervisors attending an accident prevention course. This example may be regarded as an instance of the well-known Hawthorne effect at work: where the attempt to observe something actually changes the thing that one is observing. Alternatively, this may be used to advantage as part of the training process; the knowledge that one's success at learning is likely to be assessed at the end of the day tends to concentrate the mind wonderfully.

This may be seen by some as rather manipulative, and Hesseling (1966) suggests that evaluators should explain the purpose of the research done and feed back any provisional data collected for self-analysis by trainees. This may, therefore, serve the objective of helping recipients of the training programme to achieve a gradual clarification of the process of learning. For Hesseling the facilitation of learning represents but one of the objectives that evaluation might serve. Dennis Pym (1968) is rather stronger on the correct purposes of evaluation: 'Evaluation is the backbone of the learning and change process.'

Although Hesseling suggests that evaluators should be more open about the purpose of their research, he still assumes that it is for the evaluator to decide what research is to be conducted, and for the trainees to fall in with this design. Whether evaluators, and other researchers, should have the right to impose their designs upon others has been strongly questioned by a number of authors (Reason and Rowan, 1981; Torbert, 1981). It can be argued that when learning is an explicit objective of educational research and evaluation, the research process should be truly collaborative involving both trainees (learners) and researchers (evaluators) in determining both what is to be done, and how it is to be done. But as Elden (1981) points out, this can be very time consuming, and also depends on having clear political support from those higher up the organization.

Controlling

Although Hamblin (1974) discussed control as a key aspect of evaluation, this has not received a great deal of attention in the literature. However Peter Bramley has shown (Bramley, 1991) that control is something that organizations might well impose on training managers or set up independent units especially to monitor. I became aware of this when working with Bramley on a Home Office project. This required establishment of both central and regional evaluation units to monitor the implementation of a major change in the training of junior managers such as sergeants and inspectors. Given the constitutional autonomy of local police forces in the UK, this seemed to be an indirect way of ensuring that all forces complied fully with a central policy initiative.

At first I felt this concern for monitoring was more peculiar to the police force which, like many organizations, tends to manage itself in a way that is similar to its primary purpose – in this case ensuring the implementation of national laws and controlling crime. But I then encountered similar concerns in other large organizations such as the Department of Social Security (described in more detail in Chapter 8). It is also evident that as pressures grow on educational institutions to standardize courses, and centralised accreditation becomes widespread, there is going to be an increasing emphasis on the potential that evaluation has as a controlling mechanism. Finally, with the increased competition between organizations there is a strong possibility that it will be used as a means of controlling the quality of teaching inputs provided by tutors and faculty members.

Deciding on the purpose of evaluation

In my experience it is not realistic to expect any evaluation to serve fully more than one of the four purposes outlined above, and this view is supported by Patton (1978, p. 83) who stresses the importance of being specific about purposes. This assumes, of course, that resources are limited in terms of people, time, and finance. It also provides a word of warning since it is so easy for evaluation (as with other forms of research) to be conceived on an over-ambitious scale which then results in nothing of consequence emerging from the effort involved. Perhaps it is possible for more than one purpose to be served if the questions to be answered are extremely limited, or if participants themselves take an extensive role in both the design and implementation of the evaluation. But, for normal purposes, it is important that an explicit choice should be attempted.

On the assumption that the person, or people, initiating some evaluation should attempt to clarify the purpose that their efforts are intended to serve, I have two suggestions about how they might go about this. These approaches I have labelled 'expediency' and 'interests of stakeholders'.

Expediency

The approach of expediency assumes that the given activity is under some kind of threat, and that if this is so it may be worth trying to generate some information to demonstrate the value of it. The self-diagnostic questionnaire provided in Figure 2.2 is intended to assess how vulnerable the programme might be to such threats.

Please read the following questions in relation to a particular course/programme/system etc., that you may be considering evaluating. In each case ring whichever of the alternative answers is most applicable. Remember that this is a self-diagnostic instrument rather than a highly scientific one. Its purpose is to get you thinking – so don't worry if you have difficulty making sense of one or two questions.

1   In general, how important is the existence of the programme/course/activity to those who are funding/sponsoring it?
   4 – Absolutely essential to *their* well-being.
   3 – A major priority of influential people at the present time.
   2 – Being given a certain amount of support and encouragement by influential people.
   1 – Very difficult to gauge how much support it enjoys.
   0 – Rather surprising that it's still running/happening (perhaps overlooked in last economy drive!).

2   The programme/course/activity is designed specifically to meet the needs of:
   4 – A wide range of people, most of whom are able to arrange their own funding.
   3 – A wide range of people funded by grants/awards/subsidies which look sound for the time being.
   2 – A limited population, but for whom funding is relatively reliable.
   1 – A limited population, with single source funding.
   0 – No particular group, and funding looks most uncertain.

3   How much is known of what various 'stakeholders' think of the programme/course/activity?
   4 – There is very reliable (inside) information on the views of major sponsors/funding bodies, etc., about it.
   3 – There is reasonable information about the opinions of primary stakeholders.
   2 – It is possible to make informed guesses about opinions of some stakeholders and/or a little first hand information from participants exists.
   1 – There is very little information even about what participants think of it.
   0 – It would be unwise to encourage anyone to think too much about their views of the programme.

Figure 2.2   Does it need evaluation? A self-diagnostic questionnaire (Adapted from Scriven, 1974)

4 How much information/evidence is there about the effects of the programme?

4 – Extensive information gathered from a number of sources over a long period of time.

3 – Adequate information gathered from 'reliable' informants.

2 – End-of-course questionnaire sometimes used, and action plans/projects occasionally yield some information.

1 – People (and bosses) let us know when they are dissatisfied.

0 – No one has much of a clue.

5 How well is the relationship between what goes on in the programme/course/activity and the apparent effects understood?

4 – There is extensive knowledge about which parts of the programme have an effect, which don't, and why.

3 – Participants have indicated which processes have led to which outcomes for them.

2 – There is some 'feel' for which aspects of the programme are more or less useful.

1 – It's very difficult to tell what causes what.

0 – We don't really know what actually happens within the programme/course/activity itself.

6 To what extent has the course/programme/activity been examined in relation to alternative ways of satisfying this apparent need?

4 – There is clear evidence available that it is preferable to existing alternatives.

3 – There is some evidence that it is better than the most immediate 'competition'.

2 – We know roughly what the similarities and differences are between this and alternative approaches.

1 – It is not at all clear how this compares with various alternative approaches.

0 – We have not really considered the possibility that there are other ways of doing this.

7 What do you really think those people who have had some contact with the course/activity/programme (as participants, bosses, sponsors, etc.) think about its value?

4 – It is of great value to the organization/economy/individuals in general.

3 – It is of much value when combined with the right people in the right context.

2 – It can be quite useful on some occasions, but there are plenty of other ways of achieving just as much.

1 – Many people have reservations about its value.

0 – Most people are convinced that it has no value.

This questionnaire has been prepared to help people decide whether they should attempt to evaluate a given programme. A rough guide to interpretation is that if you have ringed answers to *any* of the questions at 2 or less, your course may be vulnerable – and you should consider conducting some evaluation in that area aimed at *proving* that the thing works. If you have answered 0 to many of the questions, then it is probably not worth bothering with evaluation because the thing deserves to be wound up anyway. Although I have encountered evaluations commissioned specifically to 'kill off' programmes with which their sponsors have become saddled.

Figure 2.2 concluded

Interests of stakeholders

There are two ways of tackling this issue. The first is to identify the *main stakeholder/client* of the evaluation and to infer what purpose he or she would like it to perform. Hesseling (1966) developed his 'typology of evaluations' based on the answers to two questions: evaluation *for whom*, and evaluation *by whom*. Under the former question he discusses the objectives and prerequisites of each 'consumer of evaluation' when considering the results of training. These are as follows:

- For *trainees* it would represent 'the last stage of a continuous learning process. In this sense evaluation can be seen as the interpretation of the learner's experience with new modes of behaviour' (p. 49).
- For the *trainers*, 'the main objective of evaluation for the trainers is improvement of their training methods . . . [Their] learning from experience must be put on a more objective basis than intuition only' (p. 51).
- For those involved in the supervision and *management of training*, typically expectations from evaluation research will be 'an indication what the critical points in training programmes are and how they can judge the performance of trainers and trainees' (p. 52).
- *Policy makers*, whether in organizations or central government, will 'expect from evaluation research clarification of goals which can be reached by management training and a prognosis of the intended and unintended consequences of management training. They are interested in whether and how they have to allocate people, time and money to obtain optimal results from training programmes' (p. 52).
- *Scientists*, and professional evaluators, will expect 'evaluation studies to give insight into the dynamics of change underlying the effectiveness of the training programme' (p. 55).

Thus it is likely that trainees, and to a lesser extent trainers, will be interested in *learning*; those involved in the management of training will be more interested in *controlling*, and possibly in *proving*; policy makers will have similar interests to training managers, except probably in the reverse order; and the trainers and evaluators are most likely to be interested in *improving*.

If one can accept the basic assumptions of Hesseling's typology, there is still the problem of identifying the main client – or at least, identifying a pecking order among different stakeholders. This is a practical dilemma which evaluators invariably have to confront, and it is better to confront it earlier rather than later in a study. (A number of examples are given in Chapter 8 from my own experiences which show just how difficult this one can be to resolve, especially when the evaluator originates from outside the organization.)

The second approach is advocated by Guba and Lincoln (1989). They believe that there should be a continual process of negotiation between all stakeholders, that the concerns and interests of one group of stakeholders should be circulated to all others, that any data collection should concentrate only on issues that cannot be resolved through these open exchanges, and that all stakeholders should be involved in interpreting the results from any such investigation. Guba and Lincoln's approach is attractive because it can provide a balanced view of priorities, and it is based on a carefully elaborated philosophy, which we shall discuss in more detail later in the chapter. However, one important limitation is that it may gloss over the very real power differences that exist in modern organizations.

'Schools' of evaluation

Having thought a little about what kind of purpose the evaluation study can and should serve, it is worth considering the general approach to be adopted towards evaluation. In this area the literature is full of prescriptions, models, catch words, mnemonics and other forms of advice about how best to conduct evaluations. Rather than providing a long list, and descriptions of these approaches, I have attempted to group them into what may be termed the major 'schools of thought', and to classify them according to what appear to be the main underlying dimensions. These two dimensions, the *scientific-constructivist* dimension, and the *research-pragmatic* dimension are described below. I will then go on to discuss the main features of each of the schools of evaluation, what their limits are, and how they relate to this overall conceptual scheme.

Scientific-constructivist

This dimension involves distinctions that are essentially of *methodology*. The two extreme poles of this dimension are often referred to as distinct 'paradigms' which means, amongst other things, that they represent distinct, and largely incompatible, ways of seeing, and understanding, the world (Filstead, 1979). This is so in theory, but in practice most evaluations contain elements of each view, and therefore may be seen to reside somewhere on a more-or-less continuous dimension. Some key features of each of these extremes are listed in Figure 2.3. The 'scientific' approach favours the use of quantitative methods involving the attempt to operationalize all variables in measurable terms. These are normally analysed by statistical techniques in order to assess absolute criteria (money, ability to recall material intended to be learnt, or instances of appropriate behaviour). In particular, the scientific approach prefers preordinate designs. That is, that the focus of the

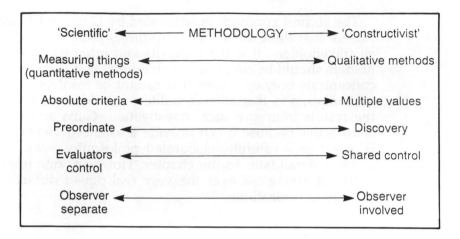

Figure 2.3 Contrasting methodologies

investigation, the measurement techniques and the ways of analysing these are determined as far as possible before any data are collected.

This aspect contrasts strongly with 'constructivist' or 'naturalistic' methodologies which emphasize collecting the views of different stake-holders before data collection begins. Appropriate reasons for the study are then identified progressively through reviewing the largely, but not exclusively, qualitative data along with the views of different stake-holders. In making sense of this data it is also assumed that it may be assessed against many different value systems, and that none of these is necessarily more valid than others.

Research-pragmatic

Whereas the first dimension of methodologies represents a debate that is extremely well worked out throughout the social sciences, the second dimension, that of contrasting styles, is of more specific relevance to the field of evaluation. The two extremes of this dimension, the 'research' style and the 'pragmatic' style, have been described elsewhere respect-ively as *E*valuation and *e*valuation (Easterby-Smith, 1980a). The former was well represented in the early writings and advice on evaluation, and the scale and complexity of research-orientated evaluation styles (which may also require significant funding and resourcing) may be one of the things that has put many people off the whole idea of evaluation.

Research styles stress the importance of rigorous procedures, whether the methodologies are essentially scientific or naturalistic. They stress that the direction and emphasis of the evaluation study should be guided by theoretical considerations (regardless of whether these theor-ies exist before, or are created during, the course of the study), and these considerations are aimed at producing enduring generalizations and knowledge about the learning and developmental processes involved. Wherever possible, the evaluator, who is normally assumed to be an independent person, is expected to maintain an objective view of the courses under investigation without becoming personally involved.

In contrast, the *pragmatic* approach emphasizes reducing data collection and other time-consuming aspects of the evaluation to the minimum possible level. This is not just a matter of idleness, however. Within companies and other organizations, most managers and potential informants are always under considerable time pressure. Hence discussions about purposes and data interpretation should be concise because one cannot presume upon the goodwill of these people indefinitely. Furthermore, as Easterby-Smith, Thorpe and Lowe (1991) have pointed out, the assumption of much social science research that the researcher is usually more powerful than the researched no longer holds when working within companies. Managers and other informants are quite capable of refusing to co-operate with evaluators, because they will always have other, more important, priorities. Evaluators therefore need to tailor their demands to the realities of the situation, making it clear that they recognize the practical interests of those involved. And if these practical interests involve helping to make good operational decisions, for example, then the evaluation study will have served its purpose once such decisions have been taken – provided they turn out to be reasonably correct in the long run. Characteristics of the two styles are illustrated in Figure 2.4.

From here it is a small step to combine the two dimensions into a matrix as shown in Figure 2.5. This has the value of enabling five major schools of evaluation to be located in a way that will facilitate discussion of their main features. In addition to locating the five schools roughly within the two dimensions, dotted arrows have been included which

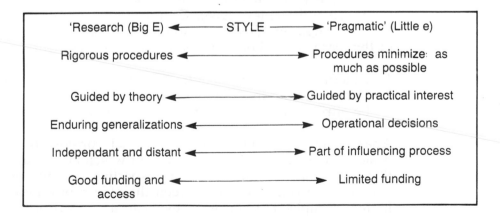

Figure 2.4   Contrasting styles

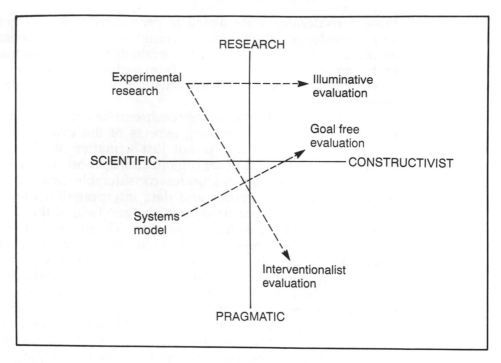

Figure 2.5 Models and 'schools of thought' in evaluation

indicate, and point to, the schools that have arisen primarily as a reaction to the school from which the arrow comes.

Experimental research

To start at the beginning, this school evolved first and has always been heavily reliant upon traditional social science research methodology. Campbell and Stanley (1966), Campbell *et al.* (1970), Kirkpatrick (1959/60), and Hesseling (1966) are some of the best known representatives of this particular school. The emphasis in experimental research is in:

1 Determining the effects of training and other forms of development.
2 Demonstrating that any observed changes in behaviour or state can be attributed to the training, or treatment, that was provided.

Apart from the emphasis on theoretical considerations, preordinate designs, and quantitative measurement which are features of the scientific and research ends of their respective dimensions, there is an emphasis on comparisons between the effects of different treatments. If, for example, the aim is to evaluate a supervisory training course which is intended to make supervisors more 'authentic' in their behaviour, the classic design would require a group of supervisors to be trained (given the treatment), and a comparable group not to be trained (receive no treatment). Individual supervisors would then be assigned on a random basis to one group or another, until sufficient numbers had been achieved. Both groups would then be measured on the scale 'authenticity', immediately before and after the training programme, and the difference in change between the two groups may then be attributed to the effect of the training programme (see Figure 2.6). There are, of course, more elaborate designs involving multiple training groups which receive slightly different treatments, and multiple control groups which receive slightly different 'non-treatments'; similarly, measurements may be taken a number of times before, during and after the training programme in question. Nevertheless, the main features are: comparisons between two or more groups, and measures before and after training.

The only problem is that it does not work particularly well in practice. For example, Hesseling provides a number of examples of this scientific research tradition being used to evaluate management training. Invariably the examples end with disclaimers, such as: 'the instruments were used and have to be tested in more situations and be refined before we can attain the accuracy and validity needed for drawing conclusions about the effectiveness of training' or 'we feel that research on a wider scale will have to be carried out in more organizations before the trainer can apply these instruments as normal tools in his work' (Hesseling, 1966, p. 113).

There are a number of reasons why this approach to evaluation does not work as well as it might, and although they apply to the evaluation of most forms of education they are particularly problematic with management training where the sample sizes are limited, and where training and development activities are often secondary to the main objectives of the organization. Four main reasons will be discussed below.

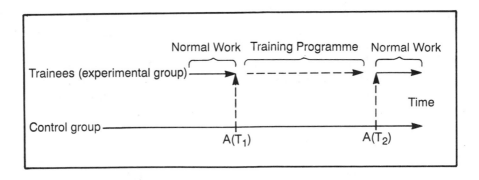

Figure 2.6 Comparative experimental research design

Sample sizes

If statistical techniques, which are essential to experimental research, are to be used with much effect, it helps if sample sizes can be quite large (hundreds, or perhaps thousands). Even in secondary schools, where potential samples would almost seem to be infinite, it is often quite difficult in practice to achieve samples of sufficient size (Hamilton, 1976). It is even more so in management training when group sizes are often less than ten, and rarely more than thirty. And this suggests that an over-reliance upon discovering statistical significances when evaluating management training and development is unwise.

Control groups

Even if it is possible to obtain samples of sufficient size to generate statistical significances, there are innumerable problems in achieving genuine matching of control groups. In companies there are decisions about whether or not to train managers with the rest of management, and they are unlikely to accept the evaluator's request for randomized selection in order to meet the requirements of some obscure research design. Careful matching between those selected for training and members of a 'control' group drawn from a larger population of managers is more feasible politically, but even then it is hard to know upon which criteria to attempt the matching. For example, in one study (Easterby-Smith and Ashton, 1975), a control group was selected by the management training manager (a psychologist) upon criteria of age, function, seniority, and assessed potential. It was not until after the results of the evaluation had been analysed that it was realised that all the managers selected to go on the programme had far closer relationships with their bosses than those who were not selected (and who thus formed the control group).

And there is a further difficulty with the notion of using matched control groups in evaluation. This is the assumption that 'no treatment', in this case no training, has a negligible impact upon those who form the control group – which is an extremely naive assumption, as those who have narrowly failed promotion boards, selection interviews, and other competitive features of the personnel machinery will be able to testify from their own experience. Indeed Guba and Lincoln (1989) now go so far as to include those who are left out, or otherwise victims of a programme, as one of their main groups of stakeholders.

Measurement

In general, there is a trade-off between the accuracy with which a variable can be measured and the significance of that particular variable. Thus it is possible to measure relatively trivial things (eye blinks, the number of words spoken) with a fairly high degree of accuracy; but outcomes that might be thought to be of rather greater importance (for example, the development of a supportive relationship with subordinates) provide greater problems. In practice, it would be necessary to reduce the latter characteristic into more trivial, and measurable, terms, such as the ratio between positive and negative comments in appraisal documents. Alternatively this characteristic might be assessed according to reports from the subordinates in question – but the purist would no doubt claim that such holistic judgements (from subordinates!) are of dubious validity. The main problem here, of course, is that the general requirement for quantitative measurement tends to produce a trivialization in the focus of the evaluation.

Causality

Although experimental designs are primarily intended to demonstrate causality between training/developmental procedures and any subsequent outcomes it is often hard to isolate these procedures from other influences on the manager's behaviour. Considerations of why a particular manager has been chosen for a 'high flier' development scheme or for a redundancy counselling programme may have considerably more effect than the nature of the programmes themselves. And although it may be possible to reduce the impact of such 'irrelevant' influences in the case of tightly structured and programmed training, as discussed in the previous chapter, it becomes increasingly hard to determine the boundaries of complex developmental programmes.

Illuminative evaluation

The normal response of evaluators from the 'experimental research' school when faced with the limited success of their efforts, is to increase the sample size, the statistical sophistication, and other features of scientific rigour. This is unfortunate (for them) because it has opened up their school to the criticisms of what is frequently claimed to be a totally distinct evaluation paradigm (Parlett and Dearden, 1981) – illuminative evaluation. Illuminative evaluation takes issue particularly with the comparative and quantitative aspects of experimental research, which are parodied in an early paper by Parlett and Hamilton:

> Students – rather like crop plants – are given pre-tests (the seedlings are weighed or measured) and then submitted to different experiences (treatment conditions). Subsequently, after a period of time, their attainment (growth of yield) is measured to indicate the relative efficiency of the methods (fertilizers) used.
> (Parlett and Hamilton, 1972, reprinted 1977, p. 7.)

Illuminative evaluation is generally used by its proponents with relatively small-scale programmes – and, as implied by the quotation above, most of these are within schools or colleges. Although there is a fairly strong commitment to qualitative research methods, the use of questionnaires and attitude measurements is not explicitly ruled out. However, there is much emphasis on adopting a flexible and open-ended approach to the research, as indicated by Ruddock's (1981) summary of the typical stages of illuminative evaluation:

> Generally, there are three stages: first, observation, further enquiry, attempts to explain; second, a progressive focus upon what appear to be key issues, often requiring extended interviews with participants; third, seeking general principles and placing findings within a broader explanatory context.
>
> (Ruddock, 1981, p. 55.)

Thus, to contrast this approach with the experimental research school, an illuminative evaluation of a management course aimed at developing greater 'authenticity' would not be greatly concerned to operationalize and measure the variable of authenticity. Instead it might focus upon the views of different people about what constitutes 'authentic behaviour' through open-ended interviews and tapes or transcripts of behaviour that was considered by some to show signs of authenticity. It might also focus upon who decided in the first place that 'authenticity' was a desirable characteristic possessed by managers in that organization, and so on. Parlett recommends that the evaluator should attempt to be a 'neutral outsider', and should recognize that there may be multiple perspectives upon any particular issue selected. Parlett also comments upon what should be the proper purposes of illuminative evaluation 'to increase communal awareness' of a particular programme and processes involved, and the evaluator should not be troubled about the need to produce specific recommendations about future actions and improvements.

It will be apparent from the above discussion that illuminative evaluation, although committed to a constructivist or naturalistic methodology, is still seen primarily in *research* terms. One reason for this is that most studies have taken place in the area of education and social programmes, where funding arrangements may be quite liberal. There are, as yet, few published instances of illuminative evaluation being employed in a managerial training programme (Reynolds and Hodgson, 1980, and Hodgson and Reynolds, 1981 being but two examples of illuminative evaluation).

However, it seems that this emphasis on *research* has led to some concern about the usefulness of illuminative evaluation amongst a number of adherents to this particular school. Participants at the third Cambridge conference on naturalistic evaluation (Jenkins, Simmons and Walker, 1981) noticed not only that this form of evaluation had proved to be more costly than anticipated, but also that an unwarrantedly high proportion of evaluation reports based on this style had during the last few years been rejected by sponsors and other clients. A number of reasons were advanced by participants at the conference for why this should be so. Firstly, it was recognized that the naturalistic evaluators' rejection of psychometric methods which provide the impression of value-free measurement had led to evaluators becoming highly involved in the politics of their studies in some instances – and this had therefore reduced the willingness of clients and sponsors to place great reliance on evaluation results. There was also a suspicion that there was a mis-match of expectations between evaluators and clients. Whereas naturalistic evaluation methods are very good at demonstrating the complexity of educational processes, many sponsors and clients who have decision-making responsibility would be hoping that the evaluation would *simplify* their task. And there was also the suspicion that whereas naturalistic evaluations generally aimed to present results in everyday language in order to improve communication, clients often show greater reverence to reports written in an alien scientific language which they do not understand. Finally, there was a feeling that naturalistic evaluation could not serve the interests of all the clients equally well.

> In practice those probably served best are the actors within the setting, who are closest to the problems and issues portrayed; the sponsors, on their account, . . . are sometimes not served well. Other audiences are served even less well. The reality has fallen short of the aspiration.
>
> (Jenkins, Simmons and Walker, 1981, p. 173.)

As with the 'experimental research' school, these problems with illuminative evaluation have resulted in some members of the school redoubling their efforts to overcome them, rather than in rejecting some of the basic principles with which they are working. It does, however, point to the possibility of other 'schools' developing which have less of a research emphasis, and consequently where the role of evaluator is more likely to be taken on by teachers, trainers, or participants. This is particularly so of the systems model which has, for a long time, been the approach recommended to management trainers.

The systems model

Although there are many different glosses on the systems model, there are three main features which occur in the writings of authors who propose this kind of approach to evaluation: a concern to start with the *objectives*; an emphasis on identifying the *outcomes* of training; and a stress on providing *feedback* about these outcomes to those people involved in providing the inputs to training.

The need to start evaluation from the *objectives* of training is stressed in *Glossary of Training Terms* (Department of Employment, 1971), although in this case use is made of the word *validation*, and a further differentiation is made between internal and external validation. Thus, *internal validation* is defined as 'a series of tests and assessments designed to ascertain whether a training programme has achieved the behavioural objectives specified'; and *external validation* is:

> A series of tests and assessments designed to ascertain whether the behavioural objectives of an internally valid training programme were realistically based on an accurate initial identification of training needs in relation to the criteria of effectiveness adopted by the organisation.

In addition, *evaluation* is 'the assessment of the total value of a training system, training course or programme in social as well as financial terms'. These definitions have been deeply ingrained in the practice of management trainers in the UK, particularly through the efforts of the industrial training boards. I must also confess that they were one of the first things that I learnt about evaluation, too. Nevertheless, the criticism was not slow in coming. Hamblin (1974) saw them on the one hand as being unnecessarily restrictive (by saying that all evaluation had to be related to objectives), and on the other hand in being over ambitious in recommending that the total value of training should be evaluated 'in social as well as financial terms'. But his own 'cycle of evaluation' is heavily dependent upon the formulation of objectives either as a starting point, or as a product of the evaluation process. Moreover his major strategies for evaluation are defined according to the level of objectives at which they commence. To do him credit, Hamblin also accepts in his model the need to look for the unanticipated, as well as the anticipated, effects of training.

A second important feature of Hamblin's work is the emphasis on measurement of *outcomes* from training at different levels. It is assumed that any training event, will, or can, lead to a chain of consequences, each of which may be seen as causing the next consequence (see Figure 2.7). The important point stressed by Hamblin at this point is that it is unwise to conclude from an observed change at one of the higher levels of effect that this was due to a particular training intervention, *unless* one has also followed the chain of causality through the intervening levels of effect. For example, it might be observed (at the job behaviour level) that a supervisor's approach to safety is markedly different from what it was six months earlier just before she attended a training programme on safety. Hamblin would argue that unless it was possible to identify what she had learnt as a direct result of the training, and unless the training related directly to the changes in job behaviour it would not be wise to conclude that the training had had this particular effect. Indeed, her change in behaviour might have been caused by a new managerial edict, by being closely involved with a serious accident in the plant, or by reading and thinking about the topic of safety for herself. Before leaving this example, it might be worth noting an interesting contrast between the relatively 'scientific' assumptions underlying the systems model of evaluation, and the way that this problem of causality would be approached by someone from the con-

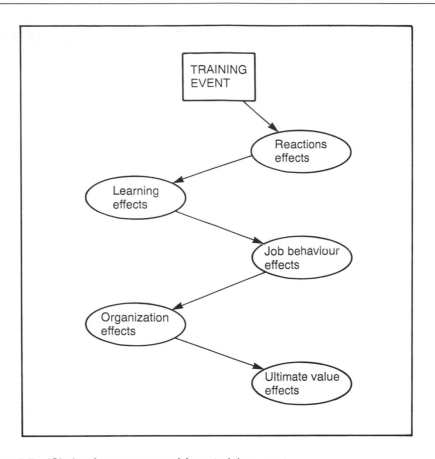

Figure 2.7   'Chain of consequences' for a training event

structivist end of the methodological spectrum. Evaluators would probably ask the supervisor for her own views of why she was now behav-
ing in a different way and then compare this interpretation with the
views of one or two close colleagues or subordinates.

The third main feature of the systems model is the stress laid upon
feedback to trainers and other decision makers in the training process.
The process of feedback from effects to objectives is an essential idea
in Hamblin's (1974) cycle of evaluation. It also features significantly in
the work of Warr, Bird, and Rackham (1970) who take a particularly
pragmatic view of evaluation, suggesting that it should be of help to
the trainer in making decisions about a particular programme as it is
happening. Most of the techniques (mainly quantitative measures) that
they recommend are relatively quick and easy to apply. Rackham (1973)
subsequently makes a further distinction between assisting decisions
that can be made about *current* programmes, and feedback that might
contribute to decisions about *future* programmes. This was a distinction
that he began to appreciate after attempting to improve the amount of
learning achieved in successive training programmes by feeding back

to the trainers data about the reactions and learning achieved in earlier programmes. What Rackham noticed was that the process of feedback from one course to the next resulted in clear improvements when the programmes were non-participative in nature, but that there were no apparent improvements in programmes that involved a lot of participation. This seemed to him to be because the content and process of non-participative programmes could be predetermined by the trainer, who was therefore in a position to use evaluative data from previous sessions in adjusting the design of future sessions. But when the programme or session was designed on a participative basis, this meant that some element of control and direction was inevitably vested in the hands of the learners; consequently its course could not be fully predetermined by the trainer, and therefore the evaluative data possessed by the trainer about previous sessions that he had run would not be so easily usable. The approaches aimed at providing feedback for decisions about the current programme and for decisions about future programmes were labelled *short cycle* and *long cycle* evaluation respectively.

The idea of feedback as an important aspect of evaluation was developed further in a later paper by Burgoyne and Singh (1977). First of all they distinguished between evaluation as *feedback*, and evaluation adding to a body of *knowledge*. The former they saw as providing transient and perishable data relating directly to decision making, and the latter they saw as generating permanent and enduring knowledge about education and training processes (see Figure 2.8).

As will be seen from Figure 2.8, these authors attempt to relate evaluative feedback to a range of different kinds of decision about training in the broad sense. The five distinct levels identified are as follows:

1 *Intra-method decisions*: about how particular methods are handled, for example 'lectures' may vary from straight delivery to lively debates between the lecturer and his or her audience.
2 *Method decisions*: for example, whether to employ a lecture, a case study, or a simulation in order to introduce the topic of 'business ethics'.
3 *Programme decisions*: about the design of particular programmes, whether they should be longer or shorter, more or less structured, taught by insiders or visiting speakers, and so on.
4 *Strategy decisions*: about the optimum use of resources, and about the way the training institution might be organized.
5 *Policy decisions*: about the overall provision of funding and resources, and the role of the institution as a whole, whether for example, a management training college should see itself as an agent for change or as something that oils the wheels of changes that are already taking place.

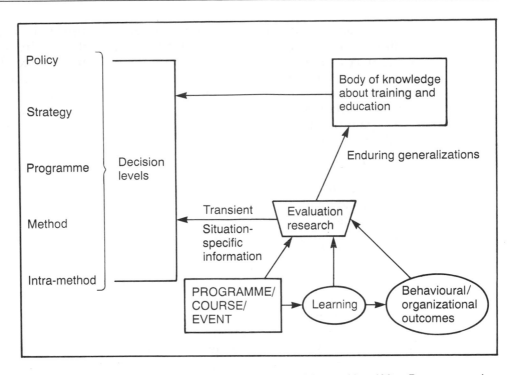

Figure 2.8 Evaluation of outcomes and link to decision making (After Burgoyne and Singh, 1977)

The above examples of applications of the systems model have all been drawn deliberately from the evaluation of training. This is because the systems model has been given such widespread application to training within the UK. As we have seen above, there are numerous examples of it being used similarly in the USA, and it has also been used quite extensively in other contexts (Rossi, Freeman and Wright, 1979). And, as will be seen in Chapter 9, it has also been used with some success in evaluating the total approach to management development adopted by an organization (Easterby-Smith, Braiden and Ashton, 1980).

Notwithstanding the widespread use and acceptance of the systems model, there are a number of problems and limitations that should be understood by those who choose to use this approach. These can be related directly to the three main features discussed above, and I shall take them in their reverse order now.

Firstly, the main limitation with the notion of *feedback* is what I call the 'systems fallacy'. This is that data provided from evaluations of what has happened in the past can only contribute marginally to decisions about what should happen in the future: logically they can only contribute to incremental adjustments based on past designs, and cannot in themselves indicate whether any more radical changes should be made in the future. For example, a systems-based evaluation of an executive programme might indicate which visiting speakers were liked, and which were not. This data is obviously useful to a programme director in deciding whether or not to invite certain individuals back to the next course; but it cannot tell him who to invite instead, nor could it tell him whether he should scrap the whole idea of visiting speakers in favour of establishing a self-developmental learning community for these executives. In order to arrive at this more radical change the programme director would need either to gather data from outside the existing programme, or to indulge in some of the more creative evaluative processes suggested by Patton (1981).

Likewise, the emphasis on *outcomes* provides a good and logical approach to evaluation, but it must be recognized that it represents a mechanistic view of learning. In an extreme form it assumes that learning consists of placing facts and knowledge into people's heads in the hope that learning will become internalized, before gradually becoming incorporated in people's behavioural responses. This view might be adequate when training salesmen in how to get a better response from 'cold calls', or accountants in how to interpret a balance sheet; but it makes little sense with some of the more complex and experiential forms of learning. What, for example, is the chain of consequences when a manager on a self-development programme suddenly realizes that his family life is being overwhelmed by the structures of his working life, and he therefore needs to establish a much greater sense of balance between the activities to which he devotes his energy?

Finally, the emphasis on starting with *objectives* brings us to one of the classic critiques of the systems approach. This is the question: *whose* objectives are they? Are the correct objectives of training defined by the organization, by the trainers, by the trainees' bosses, by the trainee, or by some external validating body? As I have indicated above these may differ quite markedly, and the 'formal' objectives of a particular programme may represent a gross oversimplification. Moreover, it is questioned by a number of authorities (MacDonald-Ross, 1973) whether there is any particular value in specifying formal objectives at all, since among other things, this might place undue restrictions on the learning that could be achieved from a particular educational or training experience.

Goal free evaluation

The issue of whether or not evaluation should start with a consideration of the objectives of training and education leads directly to the next major evaluation school: that of goal free evaluation. In particular, goal free evaluation starts from the assumption that the evaluator should avoid consideration of formal objectives in carrying out his or her work. It was Michael Scriven (1972), who was credited with proposing the radical view that the evaluator should take *no* notice of the formal goals and objectives of a programme when carrying out an investigation of it.

In practice this might involve trying to avoid contact with a programme director before and during the programme, and deliberately not looking at course brochures or proposals to validating bodies. Instead the evaluator should spend time talking to participants and other stakeholders, and should attempt to observe carefully what takes place during and after the programme. Only in this way, argues Scriven, can the evaluator avoid being contaminated by those who have vested interests in the programme – and this is essential if he or she is to form a balanced judgement about the real *value* of it.

A similar line is adopted by Deutscher (1976) in pointing out the dangers of basing evaluation studies on the formal goals of programmes. For a start, he argues, the formal goals of a programme are often framed in order to attract funding, or participants, and they may represent only a small part of what the tutors (let alone the participants) hope that the programme will achieve. If the evaluator focuses his or her attention on these formal goals the study may only pick up a small part of what actually happens on the programme. Deutscher makes three suggestions about how to deal with, what he calls, the 'goal trap'. First, he advises the evaluator to discuss with all interested parties (stakeholders) what they would consider to be reasonable objectives for the programme. This should provide a far wider basis for judging the value or otherwise, of the programme. Second, even if a range of objectives is taken into account, there is still a danger that the evaluation will concentrate on what was generally expected at the beginning of the programme to transpire subsequently, and it therefore may not notice any changes in direction if they happen during a programme. To guard against this, Deutscher advises the evaluator to look specifically for *unanticipated* outcomes. Third, he suggests that the whole concentration upon outcomes (as emphasized in the systems model) is itself unhealthy. Although some interest in outcomes may obviously be necessary, the evaluator is advised to pay greater attention to the *processes* which take place within the programme and the experiences of participants before, during and after its completion. In practice this might involve observing planning meetings, discussing with various stakeholders their objectives and expectations at different stages in the programme, mixing socially with participants, and interviewing them some time after the programme has been completed.

In view of the last point, it will be seen that goal free evaluation generally demonstrates more of a preference for constructivist methods. The implicit assumption in most discussions about goal free evaluation is that the evaluator will normally be an outsider; indeed, those individuals closely involved with the programme would theoretically find their roles incompatible with the conduct of goal free evaluation. That is why the style has been located in Figure 2.5 nearer to the 'research' end of the spectrum than to the 'pragmatic' end of the spectrum. Some readers may feel this is a gross generalization, but it does seem that goal free evaluation does not necessarily have such an important research emphasis as illuminative evaluation, and there are indeed examples of some of the principles of goal free evaluation being used in a relatively pragmatic way. Jameson (1980) provides an example of a relatively successful goal free evaluation – a course for small business people which was carried out by herself, one of the major stakeholders. Although in cases like this, as Patton (1978) points out, there is always the danger that the approach will simply substitute the evaluator's goals for those of the trainees and other stakeholders.

Like many of the evaluation styles which use constructivist methods, goal free evaluation is intended to be of relevance to 'decision requirements'; but the research assumptions implicit in this style mean that it is likely to be most useful when considering innovative programmes where significant funding is available. The emphasis on providing a counterpoint to many of the assumptions in the systems model also detracts from the concentration on involvement in pragmatic decision making by the range of approaches that have been grouped together in Figure 2.5 under the label of interventionalist evaluation.

Interventionalist evaluation

There are many labels that have been applied to evaluation approaches falling within this general group: decision orientated, client orientated, barefoot, responsive evaluation and utilization focused, to name but a few. I shall concentrate on the latter two in this section because they are reasonably well represented, and their principles are quite widely disseminated.

Firstly, Stake (1980, p. 86) helps to locate this general 'school' by contrasting a *responsive* evaluation with the preordinate approach of experimental research. A preordinate evaluation requires the design to be clearly specified and determined before evaluation begins, it makes use of 'objective' measures, evaluates these against criteria determined by programme staff, and produces results in the form of research-type reports. In contrast, responsive evaluation is concerned with programme activities rather than intentions, and takes account of the different value perspectives involved. Both of these features, it may be recognized, are shared with goal free evaluation, as described above. In addition, however, Stake stresses the importance of attempting to respond to the audience's requirements for information, and this contrasts somewhat with the attempts by certain goal free evaluators to distance themselves from some of the principal stakeholders in the programme that is to be evaluated. Stake is also more catholic in his recommendations about evaluation methods, and recognizes that 'the different styles of evaluation will serve different purposes'. He also recognizes that preordinate evaluations may be preferable to responsive evaluations under certain circumstances – for example, if clients generally wish to check upon goal attainment. And it is because this approach to evaluation is more relaxed about appropriate methods that it has been placed at the pragmatic end of the scale in Figure 2.5.

This style of evaluation is taken a little further by Guba and Lincoln (1989) by what they call *responsive contructivist evaluation*. They also refer to this as 'fourth generation' evaluation in order to distinguish it from the three earlier generations:

> *measurement* which concentrated on attainment tests for schoolchildren and was developed extensively in the first half of the century;
> *description* which concentrated on the strengths and weaknesses of a programme with the main aim of improving it;
> *judgement* which stressed the importance of making reliable assessments of the value of programmes.

'Judgement' is most similar to my notion of 'proving'. Thus there is some overlap with the terms used here; the difference being an indication of the different range of interests in evaluation when applied to schools, and evaluation when applied to management training.

As we have seen, Guba and Lincoln (1989) recommend starting with the identification of stakeholders and their concerns, and arranging for these concerns to be exchanged and debated before collection of further data. It is the aspect of exchange and negotiation between stakeholders which marks their views out from Stake (1980), and it is also this feature which is underpinned by the idea of 'constructivist' methodology. The important aspects of constructivism, for Guba and Lincoln, are: first that it rejects the idea that there is any single version of 'truth'; second, that cause and effect is not a mechanistic process, but must be inferred by different observers; and third, that multiple views of truth should be sought out as a collaborative venture between researchers and all others involved. Guba and Lincoln are at pains to avoid the separation between evaluators and those evaluated, and would like to introduce an equal say for all potential stakeholders in order to reduce the tendency for evaluation studies to become dominated by a 'managerialist' perspective. While I applaud their sentiment here, I believe it is unrealistic when conducting evaluations in most organizations where significant power differences do exist and will continue, for better or worse, to exist in the future.

Patton (1978) seems more realistic with his idea of *utilization focused* evaluation. This stresses the importance of identifying the motives of key decision makers before deciding what kind of information needs to be collected. Thus he recognizes that some stakeholders will have more influence than others, but goes further by concentrating on the uses to which any subsequent information might be put. The evaluator therefore needs to discuss with clients and other stakeholders, both before and during the course of the programme, what they want to know and how they might use different types of information that could emerge. At times this might involve guessing possible results and asking stakeholders how they would interpret such data and what they could then do with it. This draws attention to the political aspects of evaluation, which will be considered more fully in Chapter 6 of this book. With regard to methods Patton, too, is quite relaxed, and accepts that both qualitative and quantitative techniques may be appropriately used in evaluation studies.

This emphasis on prior agreement with the client may be seen to conflict with Stake's view of responsive evaluation. But it is only a superficial conflict, because Patton's emphasis on discussing the design and interpretation with the client introduces a significant responsive feature; and it is also recognized that the client may develop and reform-ulate his questions as the study proceeds. A final point about this approach to evaluation, which is discussed by both Stake and Patton is that traditional research-type reports are not necessarily particularly helpful. Clients tend to be more impressed by what is known as 'face validity' (Nunnally, 1967) than the more strictly determined notions of a scientific validity. They also tend to find reports easier to use if they are written in everyday language, as opposed to the dry scientific jargon that is used in traditional reports. This contradicts somewhat with the view expressed by Jenkins, Simmons and Walker (1981) discussed earlier, that many clients really prefer evaluation reports to be written in scientific language. Perhaps the difference between illuminative and interventionalist evaluation in relation to this point is that in addition to 'user-friendly' language the latter form of evaluation approach is also likely to be addressing directly the questions that the client would like to have addressed.

The reason why I have grouped this range of approaches, which may seem to some to be quite disparate, under the general heading of interventionalist evaluation is that there is a recognition in all cases of the need for evaluation to have the direct impact upon programmes and those involved with them. It is this form of *confrontation* which Critten (1982, p. 3) argues is the very essence of evaluation:

> Until the parties involved personally confront the data that emerges through the purposes we have described, they will be unable to *fully realize* the value inherent in that experience.

In a similar vein, Patton (1978, pp. 273–4) comments:

> Finally in utilization focused evaluation the underlying and constantly recurring analysis or interpretation issue is how to translate the findings into action . . . Utilization focused evaluation is aimed at producing knowledge that makes a differ-ence, that is actually used.

The main strengths of interventionalist evaluation approaches should now be apparent. They are likely to be perceived to be relevant by decision makers, and possibly other stakeholders, and they are also likely to be realistic about the resources required to provide usable results. It is claimed that they are more 'honest' and less alienated than other approaches to evaluation, particularly compared to those that rely heavily on scientific methods. But as we have seen above, such a claim is dependent upon how it is seen by clients and others, and their expectations and judgements may not necessarily accord with the rational views of the evaluator. Finally the interventionalist styles, particularly responsive evaluation, are more likely to be flexible and adaptive to changing situations and processes as they take place during and around a particular programme.

The potential weaknesses of interventionalist evaluation approaches are closely linked to the above strengths. One danger is that this form of evaluation can become too flexible, adapting and changing to every passing whim and circumstance, and therefore producing results and conclusions that are weak and inconclusive. Another problem is that the evaluator who tries to develop a close relationship with clients and other participants may become too involved with the programme itself, thus sacrificing some impartiality and the credibility that comes with this. This is, of course, the problem that goal free evaluation sets out to avoid. Clearly there is no definitive solution to this dilemma but it is something that the evaluator, whether an insider or an outsider to a particular programme, should be aware of and should seek to maintain in appropriate balance.

Choosing an evaluation style

By this stage the reader may be becoming overwhelmed by the range of evaluation approaches and styles that are available. However, the aim of this chapter has been to demonstrate that there are a great many starting points, assumptions and purposes that may be covered by evaluation – and that evaluators should not necessarily take a particular style for granted. What, therefore, should the evaluator do when faced with this wide range of choice, and needing to make a decision about adopting one overall approach or another?

The following observations relate to the general dimensions illustrated in Figure 2.5, and the reader might then be able to relate them to specific features of the evaluation styles described above – particularly, as I have tried to emphasize, when there exists a considerable range of approaches and methods within any single style, especially from the viewpoint of different proponents of this style (Jenkins, Simmons and Walker, 1981).

First, there is the question of the relationship between purposes and styles. It should be clear from the above discussion that there are no necessary relationships between the two, for example, a goal free evaluation or an interventionalist evaluation may be aimed at *proving*, just as much as an experimental research evaluation. Similarly, examples of experimental research might be intended to facilitate *learning* just as much as the systems model of illuminative evaluation. Nevertheless, based on the apparent values, and experiences, of proponents from different schools and styles my assumption is that studies aimed at fulfilling the purpose of *proving* will tend to be located near the 'research' end of the dimension, and studies aimed at *improving* will tend to be located near the 'pragmatic' end. On the methodological dimension there may be more concern with *proving* at the 'scientific' end, and *learning* at the 'constructivist' end.

There are other more practical considerations that might help in the choice of an appropriate evaluation style. If there is no funding available to support an evaluation activity, then there is little option but to adopt a 'pragmatic' style; 'research' styles can be extremely costly in terms of time and money. My own experience of constructivist approaches, particularly when they rely heavily on qualitative methods, is that they can be far more time consuming than some of the quantitative methods employed in 'scientific' approaches. The analysis of quantitative data can be highly automated nowadays, whereas qualitative data still requires much painstaking attention from evaluators.

Apart from this, the choice between 'scientific' and 'constructivist' approaches is often one of personal preference and expertise. The fashion has swung from the former to the latter during the 1970s, and during the 1980s it swung a little back towards the scientific approach. This is because of the tighter constraints being placed upon expenditure (in the public and private sectors) in countries throughout the world, and the consequent pressures to justify activities and programmes in terms of measurable outcomes.

However, it seems that constructivist approaches which place emphasis on multiple stakeholders are becoming both academically respectable and requested by companies that have become disenchanted with the narrowness of more scientific approaches. I shall be giving some more examples of these applications in Part III of the book.

Conclusion

The main purpose of this chapter has been to highlight key features of the wide range of approaches that may be, and have been, adopted to evaluation. It has also been stressed that there are choices to make between these general approaches, and some guidance has been given in this respect.

The next chapter will take the question of choice further, by looking in greater detail at the design of evaluation studies. A general framework will be developed for looking at design alternatives, and it will also be possible to comment on how design features would be affected by the adoption of each of the evaluation styles discussed above.

PART II

Design and methods

3 A framework for evaluation

Having discussed the general purpose and styles of evaluation that may be adopted, I will concentrate in the next three chapters on the details of evaluation designs, and on the choices to be made therein. This chapter is concerned primarily with deciding what kind of focus the evaluation should adopt for data collection, and therefore it starts with a general framework which is intended to assist choices about the most appropriate focus.

I find it convenient to distinguish between three kinds of focus to evaluate activity: people, systems, and things.

The evaluation of people and their performance is most often referred to as 'assessment', and this may take the form of examinations in the context of education establishments, or of appraisals and performance reviews within organizations. It is not my intention to discuss the assessment of people in this book since it is a vast topic in its own right. Yet it may be necessary to touch on some aspects of assessment when it is being used as indirect evidence of performance and success in the other two kinds of focus. The second, *systems*, is of more relevance in this book. The evaluation of a 'system' might involve consideration of whether an organization's overall approach to management appraisal is working as well as it might, or what effect the existence of examinations has upon the learning of a group of students on a postgraduate management course. The third kind of focus, *things*, has deliberately been left vague, since it covers quite a range from events, such as courses and workshops which are bounded in time and space, to activities such as learning-on-the-job which are much less restricted.

The discussion in this chapter will, therefore, be mainly about 'things' as the focus for evaluation, and secondly about 'systems'. However, the framework that is developed below is based on the evaluation of a relatively bounded thing such as a management training course. This is partly because it is one of the most common types of problem considered by evaluators, and partly because it leads to a generalized framework which can more easily be adapted to the consideration of less tangible focuses such as developmental activities or systems. Although there will be tangential references to these below, they will be considered in more detail in Part III of the book which considers specific evaluation applications.

What to look at?

The following framework is intended to distinguish those aspects of a programme or an event, each of which might be the main purpose for the evaluation. It is also assumed that at this stage the question as to what the data is to be gathered *about* will be formulated. There are some clear parallels between this framework and those provided by Warr, Bird and Rackham (1970), and Thurley, Graves and Hult (no date) since in both works much stress was laid on the framework which guided the collection of data. For those who are familiar with these earlier works, it should be noted that although many of the same labels are used now to describe different features of the framework they are used in somewhat different ways here – and indeed the two earlier works also have quite different meanings for some of their common terms, such as 'context'. The framework proposed here has five elements: context, administration, inputs, process, and outcomes. This, it will be seen, abbreviates into the acronym CAIPO which is of no significance whatever in itself, but which may be of some help in remembering the different features. These features are illustrated in Figure 3.1.

Context

The context of a programme or an event refers, naturally, to the circumstances outside and beyond the programme itself. Evaluation of this context might include investigating why the programme is being funded and/or run, and what the different aims and objectives of various stakeholders might be in this process. Depending on the overall purpose of the evaluation, any data gathered from various stakeholders about aims and objectives might be used to confront other stakeholders with different perceptions and values as a way of checking that the programme really is representative of different views about its purpose, along the lines suggested by Guba and Lincoln (1989). Data gathered about the context may also include a consideration of why the evaluation itself is

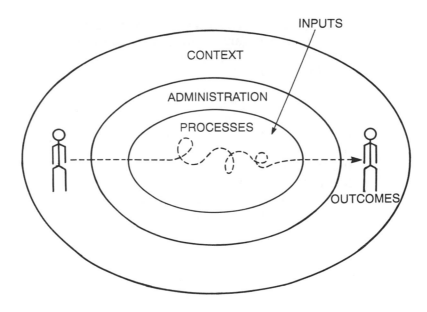

Figure 3.1 Different focuses of evaluation

being done since, particularly when extra funding and resources are involved, this is often even more political than the establishment of training and development itself.

Leaving aside political considerations for the time being, there are two basic orientations to identifying training and developmental needs for managers. The first is concerned with the *maintenance* of the present functioning of the organization, and may sometimes have a remedial flavour to it. In practice this may be done by collating developmental recommendations from managers after performance appraisals have taken place, or by the 'template' method of identifying the ideal skills for managers in the current organization, and hence designing training programmes to close the gap between this ideal state and the actual abilities and skills of managers as presently identified. Another approach is to concentrate on the nature of work performed by managers and to ask them individually about those aspects of their work that they find more or less difficult. There are many techniques and methods that can be used to identify such training needs (Stewart and Stewart, 1978); but the approach of simply asking managers for their own views leads to the second orientation, identifying training needs, which concentrates upon *developing* managers for the future. More details are given of a project that attempted to do this in Chapter 9 but its essentials require managers to identify changes that are taking place in their immediate working environments, and to anticipate the kinds of pressures that these might place upon them in future. Such views from managers 'at the coal face' as it were, can be again collated into more generalized views of the training and development needs of managers in the organization. It also should not have escaped the reader that there is here, too, a potential *learning* opportunity (Easterby-Smith and Davies, 1983).

A final way of considering the context of training and development is to evaluate *organizational cultures*, both as experienced and as desired. Roger Harrison's classification of organizational cultures (Handy, 1976), is often used for this purpose, although the results are also rather predictable (most organizations emerge with a 'role' or 'task' culture in the middle and a 'power' culture at the top; and managers generally feel that there should be more of a 'task' culture at all levels). Cultures may also be examined in more everyday terms. A result that frequently crops up is that major decisions are heavily influenced by technical considerations, and by professional groupings within an organization. For example, in modern industrial organizations there are increasing pressures to emphasize commercial and business considerations in making decisions (thus affecting the wider culture of the organization itself), and in many public service organizations, such as hospitals or schools, there is an increasing emphasis placed upon *managerial* considerations.

Administration

Evaluations that identify the context within which training and development might take place are often orientated towards general policy decisions, and may be conducted independently of any specific and developmental activities. Those more concerned with administration, on the other hand, would be directly related to specific training and developmental activities, and the decisions surrounding them. The term 'administration' as used here, is a catch-all phrase intended to address the mechanisms of nomination, selection and briefing before any training commences, and any follow-up activities whether initiated by an immediate boss or part of some post-course evaluation.

Considerations regarding the administration of training and development might also delve deeper into the reasons for managers being trained, and the processes whereby they come to be on courses. Those people with any experience of management training will know that there is a wide range of reasons why managers are sent on a training course, and these often depend on the purposes and attitudes of bosses and nominating officers. For example, four reasons that occur quite frequently are: 'it was my turn to go'; 'this person is a high-flier and the course offers a significant opportunity for development'; 'this person has been performing quite inadequately, and this course represents a last chance'; 'this person has been working very hard recently, and deserves a holiday reward'. Occasionally people even attend training courses because they themselves have requested to go – and in my experience these people tend to obtain far more benefit from their attendance than any of the other categories. Nevertheless, any evaluative attention given to such reasons can be of considerable help in *improving* training, particularly if administrative arrangements are adjusted to ensure that ridiculous contradictions do not take place – such as half the course comprising managers sent there as a reward, and half of managers sent there as a punishment; or the example I once encountered of a manager sent on a course to familiarize himself with the company's business, when he had only one more year to serve before retirement.

And then, of course, there are the administrative arrangements as normally understood in relation to training and development, and which feature regularly in end-of-course questionnaires. Thus it is not uncommon to find that on a residential programme the catering and domestic arrangements have been rated far more highly than have the educational aspects of the programme! Or, taking the emphasis away from training for a moment, the mechanics of administering an appraisal system or a job rotation scheme may well be worth evaluative investigation, since, for example, breaches of confidentiality, or apparent favouritism, may seriously be affecting their operation.

Inputs

This particular criterion emphasizes the contribution of the various methods, techniques, and people involved in management training or development. Following the distinction made in the previous chapter (see Figure 2.8), these contributions may be examined at a generalized level, or in more immediate terms. The former, which is about the potential impact of different teaching media and methods will be discussed in more detail in Chapter 7 as examples of particular evaluation applications. The latter, which features almost without exception in end-of-course questionnaires, will be discussed now.

The type of *inputs* that I have in mind might be the specific lectures, role plays, or business games on a management course, the tutors and lecturers themselves who provided and structured these, or the counselling and appraisal sessions that might be given to managers on the job. The evaluation of such inputs involves asking people to say what they thought of them – and such questions may be incorporated into rating scales or any of the range of more open data collection methods that are described in Chapter 5. This type of data is described both by Warr, Bird and Rackham (1970), and Hamblin (1974) as a form of *outcome* from training programmes (reactions data) but I think this is misleading since its use is likely to be almost entirely in modifying and changing different aspects of the programme and its staffing in preparation for the next time it will be used. This is, of course, the main reason why programme directors show a marked preference for this type of information in their end-of-course questionnaires.

Before moving on, it is worth noting that any evaluator of inputs also needs to check that the events which were supposed to take place actually did take place. For example, on a course were all the lectures and topics completed according to the syllabus or timetable, and were all those who were asked to provide comments on each of these actually present all the time? When this approach is adopted the study may also be serving the purpose of *controlling* – even more so if there is an emphasis on obtaining and collating ratings of teachers so that performances can be monitored and compared. As noted earlier in this book, such an approach is becoming more common both in the public and private sectors as competition between institutions and government monitoring becomes more pervasive. People who are asked to fill in questionnaires at the end of a course are suprisingly compliant about commenting on all they are asked to comment on. And, for example, on a recent international programme over half of the participants rated two particular sessions as being of some value when neither of the sessions had taken place – they had been invented as dummy items for the questionnaire. This point of checking precisely what took place, and for whom, is particularly important with large and complex pro- grammes involving options and different routes for participants. It is also most important for outsiders who are conducting evaluations of programmes which they themselves may not have experienced to check on these points.

Finally, another example outside the context of training is that when attempting to evaluate the effect of management appraisal systems (see Chapter 9), even in companies which have regular and well monitored appraisals, a sizeable minority of managers will always escape being appraised for one reason or another – and therefore their involvement, or lack of it, should always be checked before asking them about their experiences of appraisal.

Process

The distinction between *process* and the emphasis on inputs and outputs provided by the systems model was made in the previous chapter. Although a focus on process is not incompatible with a focus on inputs, it should be noted that evaluations which concentrate on this area tend to fall nearer the constructivist end of the methodological dimension. With this in mind, three aspects of process will be expounded in this section.

Firstly, a concentration upon process may simply involve providing a narrative of what takes place during a learning or developmental event or period. This goes a little further than just checking which sections are actually run and who attended them, as discussed in the case of inputs – although it may not involve any more than individuals keeping open-ended diaries of their participation in a one-week workshop, or keeping a tape recording of the discussion in a counselling session.

Secondly, the emphasis on process might involve trying to understand the experience of an event or activity from the viewpoint of participants, possibly based on some of the narrative data obtained as above. For example, the procedure known as protocol analysis, as applied by Burgoyne and Hodgson (1982), involves asking managers to describe their thoughts and feelings *as they were* when listening to tape recordings of discussions involved in their normal managerial activity. This particular methodology has also been used to gain access to participants' experiences of management education, particularly where it is hoped that this information will lead to an improvement in the programmes being considered. In the examples described above, there were no particular frameworks imposed on the analysis of process: in other words, any themes and issues could emerge from the data after it had been collected (Glaser and Strauss, 1967).

The third way of looking at process would involve investigating specific aspects and dimensions of what takes place, particularly in the area of interactions between people. Thus, it might be decided to investigate the natural groupings and 'pecking orders' that emerge during a residential course; the nature, and sources of, any conflicts that emerge between tutors and participants; or any aspects of the 'hidden curriculum' (Snyder, 1971) that may be established through the structures and procedures introduced by tutors and others. Information of this type is often of great value in understanding why particular courses and programmes work, or do not work, and thus might lead to appropriate changes being made 'mid-flight', or in subsequent programmes. In addition, there is also a range of structured ways of analysing interactions within programmes, particularly when it is hoped that participants will also *learn* from the experience of these interactions. Examples of these include interpersonal process recall (Marsh, 1983), and interactive skills analysis (Rackham, Honey and Colbert, 1971).

Outcomes

This is a particularly difficult area because the notion of an 'outcome' is extremely complex, and there are very many different ways of thinking about outcomes. Since outcomes (or outputs) are a crucial feature of the systems model, the most widely disseminated frameworks for understanding outcomes have been provided by those who use a systems approach to evaluation. Notable amongst these are Kirkpatrick (1959/60, 1967) (reactions, learning, behaviour, results); Hamblin (1968) (reactions, learning, job behaviour, functioning); Warr, Bird and Rackham (1970) (reactions, immediate outcomes, intermediate outcomes and ultimate outcomes). But perhaps the most useful framework for understanding outcomes is that of Hamblin (1974) which distinguishes between outcomes at the following levels: reactions, learning, job behaviour, organization, and ultimate value. 'Learning' is further subdivided into the areas of knowledge, skills and attitudes – a classification which has become very widely accepted in the training world, partly as a result of the work of Bloom and collaborators (Bloom *et al.*, 1956).

I shall not elaborate further on this schema since, even for those who have not encountered it before, it should be relatively self-explanatory. However, it is worth pointing out some of the assumptions underlying it.

First, it assumes that a training event took place before any of the given outcomes emerged; second, that the various outcomes take place within a time sequence (reactions, for example, will occur both in theory and in practice before learning takes place); third, that each outcome is, or may be, caused by the outcome that preceded it in the time sequence; and fourth, that the different outcomes are related hierarchically, presumably in increasing degrees of scale and complexity. But a number of questions can also be raised about this schema and its underlying assumptions. To start with, it begins to run into trouble if the training and development involved is not based upon a neatly bounded event or programme. For example, the outcomes of an action learning set which met for one day every three weeks, would be extremely difficult to conceptualize within this framework; indeed, it is often events within the organization, or actions (at the job behaviour level), which can become the basis for learning within a set. This also points to the fact that the assumed time sequence between different levels of outcome may easily be reversed, and there is no reason why such outcomes might not be simultaneous. One of the useful insights in the work of Kolb, Rubin and McIntyre (1971), and its development by Honey and Mumford (1982), is that individuals may learn best in different ways; some may learn from being given instruction and theory which they can then try to implement (the traditional model), while others learn from taking action, as a part of their normal jobs, on which they can subsequently reflect. Furthermore, as Ruddock (1981) points out, the assumption of causality simply because one thing takes place after another is quite misleading. Not only may there be other things which have happened between the two of them which have had a greater impact on the latter one (as Hamblin, 1974, acknowledges), but the whole association between intention and consequence, particularly if one looks at the course of human history, is exceedingly weak – and why, therefore, should one assume that there is ever a strong link between one aspect of management training and development, and another? My final reservation about Hamblin's 'chain of consequences' approach to outcomes is a little philosophical: the various terms in the five levels of outcome are really very different in nature. For example, 'reactions' are something to do with a state of mind; 'job behaviour' refers to the *activity* of people individually or collectively; 'ultimate value' implies some kind of judgement of the *worth* of an entity. Yet, as Burgoyne (1973a) points out, things like reactions and activities can be valued in their own right; conversely one may *react* to activities or to judgements of entities. The problem therefore is that these terms are being used as if they are logically related to each other, when they are in fact representative of very different categories. And this, as Ryle (1949) points out, can lead very quickly to confusion as soon as someone questions the relationships between these terms – and the different levels are not simply taken for granted. For these reasons, I believe it is worth rethinking this particular schema as discussed below.

Firstly, I find it helpful to distinguish between a person's *potential*, which may change or be affected by some form of training or develop-ment, and the *implementation* of that potential in the form of behaviour, relationships, attitudes at work, or elsewhere. This implementation is largely a function of whether the person is given the opportunity and support to make use of this potential – and is conventionally referred to as the problem of 'transfer of training'. It also represents the tran-sition in Hamblin's schema from the level of learning to the level of job behaviour. In considering the 'potential' side of the equation (see Figure 3.2) I also find it useful to distinguish between *learning* and *development* as potential outcomes.

The reason for this is that learning and development may each take place differently under different circumstances. For example, as Davies and Easterby-Smith (1984) point out, whereas managers may often learn

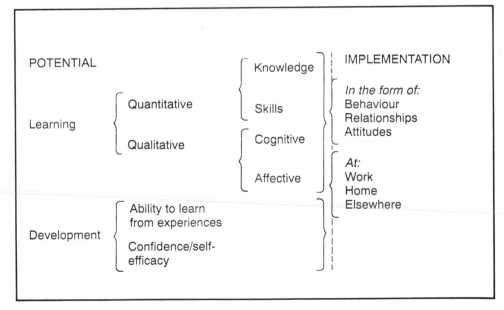

Figure 3.2 Outcomes from training and development: potential and implementation

a lot from training programmes, they very rarely seem to develop from them. On the other hand, development may be a more appropriate way of viewing outcomes from 'natural' work activities. This, in turn, is very much a function of the type of organization that the manager is working in, and its culture. *Learning* may be viewed either in quantitative terms (as the addition of more knowledge or skills), or in qualitative terms (as a matter of seeing and feeling things differently). There is perhaps some overlap between this latter (affective) form of learning, and the notion of 'development' as Davies and Easterby-Smith (1984) define it. *Development* refers more to a person's state of being, and to any changes and improvements in this. One interpretation of development (as provided by Kolb and Fry, 1975, and by Revans, 1971) is that a person's development means that he or she will have a greater ability to learn from experiences. A second aspect of development is provided by Bandura (1977) where he talks of a person's self-efficacy and general level of confidence.

It is important to remember that either 'potential' or 'implementation' may be seen as a valued end in itself. Particularly, in the case of the former, with the stress that is placed upon self-development as the major aim of much managerial training and development. There is, still, a neat twist when one considers development as a potential outcome on an individual: that people who are developing are more likely, through greater confidence and interest in learning, to create the opportunities in which they may be able to implement some of their own potential. It follows from this observation, that trainers who are concerned to achieve a transfer of whatever learning their courses are intended to provide, might also pay greater attention to development as a desirable, and necessary, outcome from their endeavours.

It is also worth remembering that the distinction between potential and implementation as used here does not necessarily imply that the latter would always have to follow the former. As Casey (1981) points out, the traditional view of the 'transfer' problem assumes that training and work occur in different times and places. This he refers to as 'transfer problem (a)' and he contrasts this with 'transfer problem (b)' which assumes that work and learning can be integral parts of the same process, and the problem is therefore one of enabling the manager to obtain the maximum learning from work experiences as they take place in such a way that this learning will naturally become part of his or her repertoire in subsequent experiences. By applying the model of 'transfer problem (b)' to the distinction between potential and implementation, it will be seen that increased potential is just as likely to follow implementation, as the other way round. (Some people may wonder why 'reactions' have not been thought worthy of inclusion in this new framework; the reason is that they have already been incorporated into one of the earlier focuses.)

Organizational change

There is another possibility which has not been fully covered by the alternative framework suggested above. This is proposed in a paper by Brewster (1981), where he is also doubtful of the value of the 'chain of consequences' model of outcomes. His proposal is for evaluations which concentrate their measures upon the wider context of the organization, and compare data gathered before with that gathered after any particular training or developmental intervention. This, he calls, 'context re-evaluation', and perhaps it should be considered as part of the context as discussed in the schema above. Although this approach does have some attraction, and may under certain circumstances provide useful additional data in an evaluation, it should be recognized that this is a very ambitious approach, and that it may also be heavy on resources. Brewster did not provide any examples in his paper of it being used to provide definite evidence of success, indeed he did not produce any examples of its application at all. Nevertheless, in a pragmatic way, the idea still may be of some value when attempting to demonstrate to appropriate stakeholders the benefits of training.

Choosing the focus

As I have indicated in the discussion above, the choice of focus may depend partly on the purpose which the evaluation is intended to serve; and it will also depend upon whether there are any particular questions to be answered. If there are not, then a fairly broad focus may be appropriate to the design of the evaluation study.

One way of using this classification of focuses is as a checklist to ensure that most aspects have been covered in a particular evaluation, especially in designing general questionnaires. The questionnaire illustrated in Figure 3.3 is one such example; and the reader might also use it to check his or her comprehension of the various categories introduced above. As an example of a questionnaire it comes quite near to the 'pragmatic' end of the scale (it took me about ten minutes to write,

---

1 What did you hope to obtain from this course?

2 Whose idea was it initially that you should come on this course? (tick one)

No idea	☐	Subordinate	☐
Boss	☐	Yourself	☐
Nominating officer	☐	Other	☐
Colleague	☐		

Figure 3.3 A sample end-of course questionnaire

3   Please tick any of the following 'subjects' that you attended during the course:

(a) Time management
(b) Interviewing skills
(c) Chairmanship skills
(d) Report writing
(e) Business environment
(f) Quality circles

(g) International perspective
(h) Budgeting
(i)   Business statistics
(j)   Grievance procedures

4   How useful did you find the following kinds of activity on this course:

	no value				extremely valuable
Formal lecture/presentations (i.e. 3(e), (f), (j))	1	2	3	4	5
Role play exercises (i.e. 3(b), (c))	1	2	3	4	5
Individual work sessions (i.e. 3(a), (d), (h))	1	2	3	4	5
Special projects	1	2	3	4	5
Informal discussions outside the 'class'	1	2	3	4	5
Interviews with tutor	1	2	3	4	5
Free time	1	2	3	4	5

5   What specific changes would you suggest to this course in order to enhance its effectiveness?

6   Were there any particular high or low points for you in this course; what do you think caused them:

	What were they?	What caused them?
High Points:		

	What were they?	What caused them?
Low Points:		

7   What was the most significant thing you learnt on this course, and what caused you to learn it?

8   Please indicate two specific things that you intend to do based on this course after you return to work.

Figure 3.3 concluded

and had not been validated before its first publication). It contains a mixture of open and closed questions; and the closed questions are both quantitative and qualitative. I would suggest that the reader notes under each question the category of focus into which it appears to fall, and possibly, why this is so.

Taking each of these questions in turn, my own interpretation, and explanations of the focuses are as follows:

1   this is mainly about *context* since it is concentrating on something *outside* the course or development activity, and it is also likely to provide one perspective on the individual's training needs.
2   covers an area of *administration* as I have defined it, since it investigates part of the mechanism associated with a person's attendance on the course.
3, 4 and 5   are primarily about *inputs*. Question 3 checks upon what inputs the individual received (and it may include dummy or redundant questions), and Question 4 concentrates upon the apparent value of different kinds of input. Some people may argue that this is a question about 'reactions' or even, 'outputs'; but whatever the label given to the judgements involved, it must be appreciated that these judgements are commenting only upon these particular kinds of *inputs*, and that is why they have been classified thus.
5   was written in order to obtain some more general comments on the *inputs* (to serve the purpose of *improving*), and is most likely to elicit comments about sessions, catering, or other aspects of how the course has been put together. However, since it is an open question it might provoke comments about selection procedures (administration), or the need for an appropriate follow-up (outputs) among some participants.
6   is intended to focus upon the *process* of the course. This is particularly so of the 'why' question, although the 'what' question might be answered in terms of specific sessions, experiences, or personal learning (inputs, process, or outcomes).
7   the first part is intended to focus on *outcomes* in the form of personal learning, and the second part of the question may produce some information either about processes, or about inputs.
8   places a clear emphasis upon *outcomes*, but it is rather different from the preceding questions in that it is intended to serve the purpose of *learning* through reinforcing whatever intentions a person may have to make use of his or her experiences on the course. This kind of evaluative focus and purpose is often employed in so called 'action plans' which are intended to improve the transferability (problem (a)) of learning from the training to the working environment.

When to look

One distinction which emerges quite clearly between scientific and constructivist methodologies of evaluation, is that with the former observations tend to take place on specific occasions, whereas with the latter observation may be seen as a more continuous process. If measures are to be made of the effect of a particular event or intervention, then it seems fairly logical for these to be made at different points in time – before, during, and after the 'thing' has taken place; and measures within each of these periods may take place at a number of times. Observations made after the course form the bulk of traditional evaluations, and these may lead to comparisons of knowledge, skills, etc., between 'before' and 'after' states, thus demonstrating the change brought about by a course in these areas. While the latter design is generally aimed at *proving*, observations made during a course may be used directly as part of the *learning* process (Rackham and Reynolds, 1971), or in order to *improve* the course as it takes place (Rackham, 1973).

If there is no particular concern to measure what has taken place, then observation and other qualitatively descriptive approaches may be appropriate. These tend to gather information on a more continuous basis, even though there are a number of ways of structuring this. One approach to this is to make observations only during specific time periods (which may be sampled on a random basis), another is to adopt the procedure known as progressive focusing (Parlett and Hamilton, 1972; Dearden and Laurillard, 1976). The technique of progressive focusing, as I have indicated above, generally involves starting with observation of a particular programme or process without concentrating on any particular feature, but as time passes the focus is progressively narrowed down to whatever topics or issues seem to be of most relevance to the purpose that the evaluation is intended to serve. This naturally begs the question of who is in a position to decide what focuses are worth investigating further, and some people would claim that the idea of an evaluator starting to observe something without *any* initial bias is also quite unrealistic. Be that as it may, progressive focusing has been, and can be, used to considerable advantage both in focusing on particular issues and problems, and in providing a rationale for switching from one to another of the focuses discussed above.

One of the 'issues' that I have been particularly aware of in conducting evaluation studies that have contained some element of progressive focusing is that the passing of time is a real factor to be contended with. This is obviously of critical importance with the more scientific designs which require pre-tests in order for the post-tests to make any sense at all (hence the stress upon preordinate designs), but it can also cause problems in constructivist design since once a given process or event has taken place, it may be very hard to recapture it (with or without the help of techniques such as 'stimulated recall'). For example, if an evaluator who is investigating the evolution of a large management programme decides near the end of the programme that the key subject to investigate is the dynamics of the faculty group, then he or she may be a little too late to start investigating that particular focus: memories are notoriously short when people are working under pressure, and notoriously distorted when these pressures come from each other. On the other hand, it still may be possible to investigate some aspects like 'nomination processes' as experienced by participants late in the day, since recall in these areas may be more reliable, and less biased.

Conclusion

In this chapter I have presented a framework to help in providing a focus for evaluation, and have discussed some of the considerations in deciding when and where to look for material. There has been a deliberate emphasis upon evaluation of courses in this chapter, partly because the concepts can most easily be illustrated in relation to courses, and partly because most of the previous, and available, literature has discussed these aspects of evaluation in relation to courses. In terms of the overall framework discussed at the beginning of the chapter, such courses form a particularly bounded form of activity (thing); there are, of course, many management development activities which are less bounded and which may be seen as processes. There is also the general focus upon *systems* which has been touched upon in places in this chapter, and which will be discussed further at a later stage in this book.

In the last section the discussion began to touch on different methods for collecting information, contrasting the more constructivist and scientific methodologies. This provides a natural lead into the next chapter which will continue the overall discussion of evaluation design by focusing upon particular media of data collection.

4 Data collection media

A general theme to Chapters 4 and 5 is the problem of capturing aspects of 'complex reality' in a form that can be recorded and communicated to others. If one has decided, for example, to concentrate on the 'process' aspects of a tower building exercise during a management course, how can one gain access to the totality of experience of all those involved? Even if multiple methods are to be used to gather data presumably each method will be able to access different aspects of that experience – but in what ways do different methods provide a selective bias to perception? Another way of considering the problem is as a process of *filtering*. Clearly it is not possible to capture everything that takes place in a group, even during a short period of time. Each choice as to emphasis and about methods represents a decision to select some, and not other, aspects for recording. Instruments such as Rackham's 'interaction process analysis' will filter out many of the observable behaviours (mainly verbal) but they will miss most of the non-verbal behaviour, feelings and emotions that take place. Other approaches, which will be discussed later in this chapter, facilitate access to feelings, but are poor guides to verbal behaviours. Therefore, the choice of particular methods of data collection will largely determine what will, and will not, be seen by the evaluator.

When seen as a matter of choices there is an earlier choice before selection of specific methods and techniques – that of the *medium*, or channel, to be used for data collection. Essentially, there are three kinds of media that may be used: direct *observations* by the evaluator of what is taking place as it happens (with the assistance of tape recorders, if necessary); accumulated *records* about what has taken place in the past;

and *informants*, in other words, any people involved with the subject of the evaluation who might be able to indicate what has happened, is happening, or will happen in the future. The use of there three media, and associated issues to do with selection and sampling, will be discussed in this chapter and followed, in Chapter 5, by a review of some of the main data collection methods that can be used in evaluation.

Observations

Any competent teacher or trainer will already be a skilled observer of what is taking place in classroom: he or she will notice who is contributing and who is not, and will also be able to pick up a lot of the non-verbal cues. Similarly, a competent manager will be a skilled observer of what takes place in meetings, interviews, and other interactions with people at work. What is the difference, therefore, between 'observation' as a part of evaluation, and the observations of skilled practitioners in the normal course of their work?

There is, as ever, no sharp distinction between the two. Rather, it is a matter of degree. Two features tend to be more characteristic of evaluation observations: firstly, the existence of some conscious discipline, plans, or rules about what should be observed, and how this should be done; and secondly, the existence of procedure(s) for recording these observations. These will now be discussed in a little more detail; but before doing that it is worth considering briefly the role of the observer in all of this. This role may vary from that of being a full participant who does a bit of observing on the side, to a complete observer who plays no part in the course or programme under consideration (see Figure 4.1).

In the former case the observer will be accepted as a full participant (or tutor) by other participants, and they would often not be aware that he or she is also making some systematic observations of what takes place. An example of this would be the trainer or participant on a management course who covertly makes notes of what takes place, and then uses these notes subsequently as the basis for an article or report about the course. This is quite a common procedure when a company

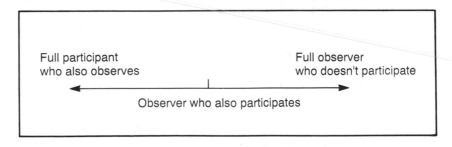

Figure 4.1   Roles of the observer

wishes to sample an open management course before deciding whether to send a significant number of managers on it – and from my own experience it is quite unnerving to discover that a participant on a course is there not to learn (or whatever), but to evaluate!

At the other end of the continuum are the observers who take no part in the proceedings themselves. They are either presented to participants as observers (perhaps experts, or top managers), or they are hidden behind two-way mirrors. When operating specifically as observers, evaluators are unlikely to obtain access to the 'inside information' that a participant observer will be party to, and they will find it hard to empathize with the feelings and emotions of those involved in the event or activity itself. On the other hand they are less likely to experience personal dilemmas, and their task may be less time consuming than that of participant observers.

Whatever the role of the observer, it is not possible to observe everything that takes place, and the observer must either start with, or develop subsequently, some way of selecting what to observe. Those who favour the more qualitative and constructivist methods tend to advocate a *holistic* approach to observation: that is, the observer does not attempt any focusing or filtering initially, and merely records whatever takes place. After some time the observer may choose some aspects that are apparently of importance to the programme, and this may form part of a gradual and continual focusing process. One should also note that in most cases it is the observer, not the participants, who decides what the focus is to become. An example of this holistic approach is provided by Reynolds and Hodgson (1980) where one of the authors participated in a research training programme, and explicitly interviewed other participants as the programme progressed. Although starting with a general interest in the 'learning milieu' and the effect that this had on the course and its participants, the authors began to concentrate on a specific contradiction in value systems which seemed to be causing a number of problems. This conflict was between the need to maintain a positive and supportive (non-critical) atmosphere in the learning event, while learning to operate within a research culture which traditionally is detached, analytic and critical. The authors were then able to present this particular dilemma to participants towards the end of the programme as part of the wider learning experience.

The evaluator in the above example joined the course without any clear frameworks within which she intended to make her observations (and this could account for the success in chancing upon a very significant problem), but it is more common for evaluators, particularly those of a more 'scientific' persuasion to adopt a *selective* approach to observation.

There are numerous bases for making selective observations, and I will mention four here: sampling by time, by incidents, by people, and by analytical categories. *Time* sampling is frequently used when observing the behaviour of individual managers or supervisors in order to understand what their jobs involve, and hence perhaps as a basis for deducing training needs. One of the methods employed by Hamblin (1974) requires the observer to look at the subject for short periods of time occurring at random and to categorize the apparent behaviour of the individual during that period (i.e. walking, talking, giving instructions, listening to others, writing, etc.) The frequency of each activity recorded from a large number of observations over a period of hours or days will indicate the overall percentage of time that an individual spends in each activity. In theory this form of observation can be used when the evaluation is aimed at *proving*, to see whether a training programme has changed the overt behaviour of trainees between observations made before and after the training. Naturally this says little about whether the *meaning* of that behaviour has changed in any way – although some observers also try to overcome this limitation by asking subjects what they are doing at the time of the observation (Thurley and Wirdenius, 1973). A similar process of time sampling may also be used within training sessions where it is wished to capture thoughts or feelings of participants. Thus members of an audience might be asked to write down one word describing their feelings every ten minutes during a lecture. This form of data, when collated, can be quite powerful as an instant barometer on the mood of a class – but it has the drawback of intruding into the process that it is intended to monitor.

On the other hand it is unlikely that a pure observer, who was avoiding intrusiveness, would gather much information of value if the sampling was purely on a time basis. A more deliberate approach to sampling would be necessary, and this might be provided either by specific incidents or specific people. *Incident* sampling involves looking for crucial episodes or incidents which might have a significant impact on the development of the course or programme – such as heated exchanges between participants, of slips of the tongue and other mistakes by a tutor. *People* sampling involves concentrating on a limited number of those involved on the assumption that they will either be representative (as with random sampling), or informative (as with purposive sampling), about the population from which they are drawn. Thus, if one wished to evaluate the operation of a career development system which provided differential treatment for those classified as high flyers compared to other managers – one could either observe individuals at random (say, every third name on a list arranged alphabetically), or purposively (say, by concentrating on the 10 per cent of the group who just *failed* to be classified as high flyers).

Finally, there are observations sampled according to *analytical categories*, such as physical location, or verbal interactions within a group. It is only the actions, or whatever, which fall within the chosen observational framework that are recorded, and everything else is ignored. Consequently this approach can give a highly focused impression of what takes place, but it is necessarily a partial one. One classic series of observational studies was carried out by Bales (1950) on the interactions between members of a group. The 12-category scheme (see Figure 4.2), which Bales initially developed after observations of group discussions held by the successful Alcoholics Anonymous organization, involves attempting to classify every statement into one category or another (it is therefore more intensive than time sampling which only records what is taking place at particular times). The categorization was conducted by hidden observers, and the results of this exercise were used to demonstrate the effect of group experiences upon the behaviour of members (an evaluation aimed at *proving*).

Positive	1	Shows solidarity
socio-	2	Shows tension release (jokes, laughs)
emotional	3	Agrees (understands, complies)
Gives	4	Gives suggestion (direction)
task	5	Gives opinion (analysis, feelings)
help	6	Gives orientation (information, classification)
Requests	7	Asks for orientation
task	8	Asks for opinion
help	9	Asks for suggestion
Negative	10	Disagrees
socio-	11	Shows tension
emotional	12	Shows antagonism

Figure 4.2   The interaction process analysis categories observed by Bales (1950)

This scheme developed by Bales for analysing interactions in groups has been adapted in numerous ways for looking at groups of managers, some more, or less, elaborate. For example, Stewart and Stewart (1978) employ the following categories in analysing behaviour in groups: proposing, supporting, building, disagreeing/criticizing, seeking information, giving information, and other. And it is not too difficult to devise other schemes for particular purposes. One such scheme was devised by Binsted and Snell (1981) in their study of the behaviour of management teachers in relation to the learning outcomes of different forms of learning event.

One feature that has become increasingly common in management training is the feedback of interaction analysis to trainees as part of the process of encouraging them to try out new forms of behaviour. In evaluation terms, the purpose here is swinging from *proving* to *learning;* and participants themselves are often expected to carry out their own observation of themselves and others as part of the learning process. In my own work as a faculty member on the International Teachers' Programme, an annual summer school run in Europe for management teachers in business schools worldwide, I used to provide a checklist of types of interaction, and all participants in the audience (who were themselves lecturers in management) were asked to look for one example of each type of interaction established by the teacher during a short lecture (see Figure 4.3). Not only did the teacher discover a little of how he or she was perceived by others, but the exercise also gave the audience practice in the skills of observation and providing feedback.

Try to recall specific examples from the lecture to illustrate some of the following:

1 A clear explanation of a point – how was this done; what use was made of examples/illustrations?
2 An explanation of a point – how was this done; what use was made of examples/illustrations?
3 Summarizing something in the middle of the lecture before moving on to the next point.
4 Use of pauses and/or silence.
5 Bodily activity: one time when (s)he was very active; another time when (s)he was very still.
6 Variations in tempo and themes.
7 Other approaches to maintaining interest and attention: jokes, stories, games, etc.
8 An attempt to gain involvement from the audience. How did (s)he do it?

Figure 4.3 Observational checklist for delivery/intervention during a lecture

Recording observations

When observations are being carried out selectively, and particularly when categories for analysis are predetermined, the problems of recording the observations are not too great. But with holistic approaches to observation, and some of the 'selective' approaches some forethought is necessary, and perhaps some training is advisable for those who will be conducting observations. It is important that observations are recorded in writing as soon as possible after the event, and when making these notes there are a number of conventions that should be followed. Patton (1980) provides four general guidelines for recording qualitative observations.

1 Notes should be descriptive rather than interpretative. Thus: 'the student stammered when he replied, his face was unusually red and his right hand was trembling', rather than 'the student replied angrily'. In other words sufficient (neutral) detail should be provided so that others can decide for themselves what the data mean.
2 Speech should be recorded as *proper quotes* whenever possible, and quotation marks should be used in the notes when this is appropriate.
3 When the observer is also a participant his or her *reactions and feelings* about what takes place should be included.
4 Tentative *insights and interpretations* (by the observer) should be

included in the notes, although, as with the above point these should be clearly distinguishable from the direct observational notes (perhaps use square brackets or some other convention).

These guidelines were devised for observers carrying out evaluation *research*, where it is important that notes are in a form that are clear to other researchers; but some of the above points about taking notes of observations may also be of use to trainers and others who wish to carry out observations as part of pragmatic evaluations.

Not that observations will always need to be recorded in writing. Small dictaphones can be very useful for recording observations afterwards. Indeed the researchers' technology reached its apogee with the invention of the Stenomask which allows the observer to dictate directly into a microphone without anyone around being able to hear what is said. This seems to be the ultimate in quasi-covert observations!

Records

As Patton comments:

> In contemporary society all programs leave a trail of paper that the evaluator can follow and use to increase knowledge and understanding about the programme.
> (Patton, 1981, p. 152.)

This points to a large amount of information that may be available at a fraction of the time, expense, and effort required for observations. The heading 'records' is used here in the broadest sense to include any enduring traces left behind by a course, programme or activity, and which could subsequently be available to an evaluator. One of the main distinctions to be made between 'records' and 'observations' is that the former do not give the evaluator any influence over the selection of what is to be recorded, and in most cases their accumulation is quite independent of any evaluative activity. Nevertheless, the problem of selection and interpretation from among these records remains.

First of all there are the records on paper. If it is a management course that is to be evaluated there may be proposals and draft outlines for the course, letters between tutors and clients, nomination forms for participants, internal memoranda justifying expenditure involved by the course, jottings on notepads, comments written on flipcharts, and so on. The operations of a potential assessment system in a company may leave a multitude of reports, ratings, records of career development interviews; numerous working documents about the establishment of the system initially; and a stack of comments and reports from the last occasion when the system was reviewed and revised.

There may be considerable difficulties in gaining access to such material – difficulties both moral and political – but this may be no justification for not attempting to gain access. My own experience of conducting evaluations as an outsider bears this out. On two separate occasions I have been employed by organizations to conduct evaluations of management development activities only to discover halfway through the project that complete evaluations of the same activities had already been carried out by other investigators. In organizations that are either highly secretive or rather forgetful this may simply be an error. But often as not the second evaluation is being commissioned by one interest group in order to counteract the effects of the previous evaluation commissioned by another group. In these cases it is quite understandable that some of the facts will be concealed, and evaluators, particularly when they come from the outside, would be well advised to exercise their investigative skills. For insiders or outsiders, access to any such existing records and data can save much time, and may be extremely illuminating.

Apart from obvious paper records there may be other 'free' information which falls into the category of 'unobtrusive measures' (Webb *et al.*, 1967). To acquire such information may require some ingenuity on the part of the evaluator, and interpretation may be a little difficult. However, on a residential management course there may be some significance in:

- the amount of notepaper taken by participants from the stationery store;
- the level of takings at the bar (and nightly fluctuations);
- the amount of time spent by participants calling home; or
- the number of handouts (and books belonging to tutors) that disappear.

Similarly, with an appraisal system based on a new form completed both by appraiser and appraisee, there may be some significance in the ratio between blank forms issued and completed forms returned; or in the timing and frequency of inquiries to the personnel department about how to fill the forms in.

Finally there is the growing array of technological records that are available: audio tapes, video tapes, and photographs being three of the most commonly used forms. It may be possible to persuade participants in crucial meetings (from which the evaluator has been excluded) to leave an audio, or even video, tape running, and sometimes sessions – particularly on training courses – will have been recorded as a matter of course. If it is vitally important to the evaluator that the given session or activity is recorded, then it would be unwise to trust purely to recordings. Technology goes wrong far more frequently than the technical specifications would lead one to expect. The heat of the moment and the desire not to intrude on the processes to be recorded means that basic precautions such as checking at the start that the machinery is recording properly are often overlooked.

It is also important to remember that all technological records will present only partial pictures. Not everything can be included in the field of vision of the video camera; and even within the field of vision not all will be revealed. Even still photographs, as Becker (1979) points out, can be highly misleading. Photographs may be faked deliberately; more often they simply reflect the selectivity of the photographer according to what he or she thinks is important – either in the subject, or in the photograph. In addition there may be problems of access which result in negotiations about what should and should not be photographed. An example given by Becker is from his own photographic recording of medical teams working at rock concerts in the USA. One of the conditions laid down by teams was that he should not photograph any patient's face. While this provides an obvious protection of privacy, it also limits the conclusions that can be formed from these records.

Informants

The feature that distinguishes the use of informants from the preceding two is that the researcher or evaluator becomes dependent upon information provided by another individual, and in providing this the informant will inevitably be making some form of judgements. This is so even when the informant is considered to be naive and irresponsible, because even psychometric tests require the subject to exercise some judgement in responding to questions – and it is precisely because this judgement is exercised in different ways by different individuals that the tests have a value.

What kind of informants?

One of the first questions to consider, then, is to what extent the informant has direct experience of what is being evaluated, and from what perspective this is being gained. These perspectives are classified in this section into four main groups: 'direct participants', 'observers', 'controls', and 'stakeholders'. The groups are not all mutually exclusive and in some cases the boundaries are indistinct; but they range on a rough continuum from those who have close and direct involvement to those who have little or no direct contact with the course or programme.

Firstly, *direct participants* are those who are either the targets or agents of the programme in question. On a management training course this would include all delegates (students) and all tutors involved. Depending upon how the course was conceived and defined this might also include, to a lesser extent, bosses and a few other colleagues at work. The direct involvement of bosses is one way of tackling the 'transfer of training' problem, and may form a necessary part of programmes that rely substantially on the use of projects (Ashton and Easterby-Smith, 1978). But participants themselves are likely to have the most extensive information, and may be able to cover any of the five focuses discussed in the previous chapter.

Participants may also be capable of distancing themselves from the action and commenting as observers upon what has taken place. Bosses, subordinates and colleagues are often regarded as good observers of the outcomes of management courses; likewise secretaries and clerical workers may be good observers of the actual operation of management development systems. Within educational establishments, people who provide student services such as counselling, students' unions, or academic tutors may be well informed as to how courses are experienced – and the possible implications of confidentiality should not necessarily discourage the evaluator from asking! Indeed there are a surprising number of decisions made and judgements formed through chance encounters with observers in bars and social gatherings. Such 'observers' are not usually trained in observational skills, as may be the case with evaluators who are using observational methods; indeed, it is the casualness of these observations and the detachment of the observer which seems to lend such great credibility to this kind of information.

There is also a special kind of observer who might be called a 'key informant'. In my early days of research and consultancy I was occasionally fortunate enough to encounter people who had no formal link with my project but who had some privileged access to information. These people may be sufficiently perceptive and helpful to explain and interpret things that are otherwise incomprehensible to the outsider. It was from such key informants that I learnt why one particular project was stopped (because another senior manager had just won a battle with my sponsor over who was authorized to approve expenditure on major personnel projects), and why another one was given funding (because the managing director was trying to close that department down, and one of the ways of resisting that was to use existing budget allocations to gather evidence to rebut his attacks). Key informants may not always be right and they may be working their own agendas, but interpretations like this can give an outsider vital leads which can always be checked in other ways. Because of this I am always on the lookout for potential key informants when starting work in a new organization!

Somewhat different issues are raised by the delineation of *controls*, who form the third group of informants. In theory a 'control' should be identical in every way to the participant ('experimental' subject), with the exception that the control does not receive any 'treatment'. This notion works very well with seedlings that are to be given various treatments, and quite well with rats (provided that they are of the right strain), but with managers and other adults there can be problems. First of all most companies are not sufficiently indifferent to training and development to allow random allocations and not uniform enough to enable adequate matching of managers; nor are the resulting groups of controls and experimental subjects likely to be sufficiently large to make statistical analysis of results particularly conclusive. Although statistical tests appropriate for small samples exist (Siegel, 1956), groups comprising hundreds, or thousands, may be necessary to reach the levels of statistical significance required by the scientific methods that advocate the use of control groups.

Another problem with the use of control groups is highlighted by the well-known 'Hawthorne effect'. This was first recognized during some experiments in manipulating the working environment in an electrical components factory in Chicago. Levels of productivity were monitored in two identical units of the same factory, where conditions such as lighting intensity and breaks were varied from time to time in one unit, but not in the other. Researchers were puzzled to notice that productivity increased steadily in the experimental unit regardless of what environmental manipulations were currently in force; they were even more puzzled to discover that increases in productivity were mirrored in the control unit where no environmental changes had taken place. The conclusions drawn from these results by the human relations movement in industrial psychology is that people will work harder when they feel someone is taking an interest in them and their work (Schein, 1970). For our present purposes, this example provides one demonstration of how hard it may be in an organization to isolate one group of people as controls to compare with another group receiving an experimental treatment.

It is therefore unwise to assume that 'no treatment' is the same as 'non-treatment'. Management development and personnel policies can rarely afford the luxury of random assignments to one group or another, and the non-selection of a manager for training may have just as much effect on him or her as selection. As remarked earlier, this may be of particular significance when it is a question of being selected, or not, for fast-track career progression. Nor should managers be considered simply as passive recipients of whatever development is meted out to them. One of the conclusions from an evaluation study using repertory grids before and after a project-based management development programme was that members of the 'control group' seemed substantially to have consolidated their relationships with their bosses while the chosen group of trainees were away learning apparently weird and irrelevant things at a business school. (This is, of course, a slight parody! However, further details of this project are given in Chapter 5, and in Easterby-Smith and Ashton (1975).)

The final group of informants I have labelled *stakeholders*. Although most of the above groups can be considered as stakeholders in one way or another (i.e. they have some legitimate interest in whatever is the focus of the evaluation), my concern here is with those who do not have any direct contact with the programme (or quasi-contact, as in the case of control group members). First of all there are 'institutional' stakeholders, such as the top managers who authorize expenditure on particular forms of programme, the government ministers who author- ize funding of major social and educational programmes, or the senates of universities which authenticate degree schemes as being of adequate academic standard. These are all stakeholders in the sense that they may be held accountable if they are shown to have made the wrong decisions, and although they may not have direct contact, they are all likely to have reasonable channels of information about what is taking place. As such they should not be overlooked, particularly since they may give more credence to their own channels of information than to the results of an evaluator's investigations.

There are a number of other stakeholders who *are* invariably over- looked because they have neither obvious informational value nor politi- cal relevance. These may include wives, husbands, children, customers, secretaries, or future employers (for students). The latter three may be able to provide crucial information (opinions) about the outcomes of an educational programme; the former three may be crucial informants about the process of the programme. Also, reflexively, they may have a major impact upon what their respective husband, wife or parent may be getting out of the programme. This is very noticeable on part- time academic courses where spouses have repeatedly to cover domestic arrangements during residential weeks, to put up with nervous depressions when essays are being written, and occasionally to accept financial privations so that fees can be paid. These people not only have a considerable personal investment in the programme, they are also likely (they certainly have the right) to be well informed about what takes place.

Some examples of the various kinds of informant discussed in this section are summarized in Figure 4.4. Readers might like to try formula- ting their own lists based on their own programmes and activities (a consideration of the part-time MA in Management Learning at Lan- caster University yielded a list of 34 categories in the stakeholder column alone).

Direct participants	Observers	Controls	Stakeholders
Trainees	Bosses	Would-be trainees	Top managers
Registered students	Researchers	or students	Funding bodies
Bosses	Colleagues	who aren't	Government agencies
Personnel specialists	Secretaries	studying	Accrediting bodies
Tutors	Clerical staff		Husbands
Academic staff			Wives
			Children
			Clients
			Customers
			Future employers

Figure 4.4 Examples of informants for evaluation studies

Selection of informants

Approaches to selecting informants may be ranged roughly along the *scientific-constructivist* continuum: from those who advocate *random* selection to those who advocate *purposeful* selection – and there are a number of intermediate positions too (Patton, 1981). The main reason for adopting random selection of informants is to enable generalizations to be made from a sample of people to the population from which that sample is drawn. The obvious examples are in political or consumer surveys when decision makers wish to find out with minimum cost what very large numbers of people may be thinking, feeling, or intending to do. Random sampling is also appropriate in some educational evaluations when numbers may be very large (say, a comparison of the attainment of children in mixed sex schools compared with children in single sex schools). But even then randomness may be difficult to achieve in practice when one considers the variety of schools that can exist in countries that apparently have standardized education systems – to say nothing of the politics of gaining access to institutions and individuals.

Within large organizations it may be more appropriate to use a random *stratified* sample in order to gauge feelings on a particular issue. This approach is used in large companies with the Management Development Audit (see Chapter 9) and involves segmenting managers into departments, or other appropriate units, and then selecting managers within those departments by random means (one means of random selection is to take every x^{th} name on a list of names arranged alphabetically, the first name being selected from a table of random numbers). The point about a random stratified sample is that the percentage selected from each department or unit can vary to ensure that adequate numbers are covered in each unit. For example, if there were 500 people to be surveyed in the production department, but only 50 to be covered in the marketing department, then the percentage sample would be very much greater in the latter case than in the former. Of course these varied sampling fractions should be taken into account when collating results across units of different size.

In the case of management training courses, the numbers will not normally be sufficiently large to make random sampling procedures of much value; indeed there is little reason to bother with sampling when the total population to be considered is only ten or twenty. This is the 'scientific' justification for distributing end-of-course questionnaires to all participants at the end of management programmes. The other justification is that most managers see it as their *right* to provide some assessment and feedback, and would be highly cynical about over-elaborate sampling procedures.

When a particular course is frequently repeated there are several other options available for evaluators. One approach is to take a 'cohort' (all participants about to attend the course when the evaluator arrives on the scene) and to follow this cohort intensively before, during and after the programme. This is sometimes referred to as a 'longitudinal' study; the obvious drawback being that it takes a long time to complete. A more cost-effective option, which we have adopted in several evaluation studies at Lancaster, is what we call a *quasi-longitudinal* design. This involves selecting several groups of managers: one before attendance on the course; one currently attending it; and one or two some time after attendance. The evaluator is then able to gather data from managers at different stages in what is assumed to be the same experience – all within the same few weeks. Indeed, when a particular course is highly standardized, it is likely to be the standardized product that is of interest to the evaluator's clients rather than the operation of any single course, and in this case it may be appropriate to do random sampling of *courses* for evaluation.

The above instances of random sampling or selection of total cohorts or populations are feasible because groups of participants, tutors, bosses, or whatever, can be quite clearly defined. When the population is less clearly defined (as with the range of possible stakeholders who may be involved) it is necessary to adopt more *purposive* sampling strategies unless one simply takes the first people who come along (known as a 'quota sample' by researchers.). Also, when populations are sufficiently large for random sampling to be feasible it may be much more effective and accurate to adopt a purposive sampling strategy.

Patton (1981) discusses six different ways of sampling purposively:

1 *Sampling extreme or deviant cases*, who may be particularly troublesome or enlightened about what is taking place.
2 *Sampling typical cases*, who are so obviously average and unexceptional that data gained from them will be given high credibility.
3 *Maximum variation sampling*: picking people who represent different points on some important continuum (say, age) so that representativeness can be demonstrated along that dimension (this is a less formal instance of the random stratified sampling.
4 *Sampling critical cases* where it may be concluded, 'if the course works for him, it *must* work for everyone!'.
5 *Sampling politically important or sensitive cases* by gaining an interview with the personnel director so that he or she becomes more aware of what is going on, or remembering to include the chairman's latest protégé in the interview sample.
6 *Convenience sampling* which involves taking the easy cases, thus saving time, money and anxiety.

No doubt the pragmatic evaluator, or the busy trainer evaluating his or her own course will be tempted to opt for the last of these approaches; but depending on the context and needs of the evaluator several of the other approaches may also be adopted to advantage.

Returning to the four kinds of informant discussed above, it is likely that random approaches to sampling will be adopted, if at all, with groups of participants and controls; purposive sampling is more likely to take place with observers and stakeholders. Where there is a clear choice in the basis for sampling, the strengths and weaknesses of each extreme should be recognized. Random sampling, provided the rules are followed carefully, should guard against any systematic biases, and should enable results to be analysed statistically. Purposive sampling allows for more precise investigation and may provide a stronger safe-guard against bias particularly when groups are small and informants are highly varied. It does require slightly more skill if it is to be done well and some additional justification of its validity may be necessary if reports and recommendations are to be provided for clients who may have been schooled in the more scientific traditions of research.

I conclude this section with an example from an evaluation of technical training programmes for junior managers in the Ford Motor Company.* This shows how the idea of different stakeholders (in this case *all* interested parties are labelled as stakeholders) can be combined with the provision of different sources of information to develop a series of questions for an interview-based study. A matrix was drawn up, with categories of stakeholder listed across the top and the five types of information listed down the left-hand side.

Each category of stakeholder was assessed as to what kinds of information they might provide and what questions they might want answered. The resulting matrix is shown in Figure 4.6 (see pp. 76–7), where it will be seen that kinds of information vary considerably with each stakeholder group, although there are also a number of areas of overlap between different stakeholders.

A series of interview checklists was then derived from the matrix. These checklists were used to guide conversations with different stake-holders (see examples from checklist for bosses of trainees in Figure 4.5). The procedure not only enabled the researchers to be confident that they were covering the necessary range of topics, as far as one can be sure at the beginning of a study, it also enabled them to check that they were obtaining data from sufficiently diverse sources without unnecessary duplication. Similar approaches are being used elsewhere in Ford. For example, Baines (1992) adapted the method of Guba and Lincoln (1989) to investigate the views of different stakeholders about a national graduate training programme. Baines concluded, rather along the lines of comments in Chapter 2, that their highly 'open' method-ology needed to be supplemented by a degree of quantitative analysis and by some recognition of organizational objectives.

The example is intended to demonstrate how the models described in this chapter can be put to practical use. In the following chapters we will consider in more detail some of the principles underlying the

---

* I am grateful for the contributions of Val Stead (Lancaster University), and Gordon Simmonds, Geoff Johnson and Bob Pluck (Ford) with whom I worked on this project.

GENERAL
1   Do you know much about the MSc Programme for Advanced Automative Engineering?
2   What kind of contact have you had with the programme?

OBJECTIVES/CONTEXT
2   What do you see as the main objectives of the programme?
24   What role does the course play in relation to company staff development?

INPUTS AND PROCESSES
8   If you could make any changes to the course what would they be?
12   Are there any elements missing which you think should be included?
14   Do you feel that the course is too long, not long enough, just right?
15   Are you satisfied with the course design i.e. full time residential blocks, or would you prefer a day release or other system?

ADMIN
7   What role, if any, do you have in the selection procedure?
8   What kind of role should managers of course participants play?

OUTCOMES
1a   How would you rate the overall value of the course? (Examples)
14   Can you give two specific examples of how the participant was able to apply their learning at work, during and following the course? (Prompt for knowledge, skills and attitude)
15   Can you give examples of how the participant might be able to make use of their learning in the medium and long term? (Prompt for knowledge, skills and attitude)
16   How do you see the participant's present and future career development as a result of this course?

Figure 4.5   Sample interview checklist for trainees' bosses

construction and use of interview checklists, and other methods of data collection.

Conclusion

Although it may be felt that the points in this chapter about different media and their sampling are somewhat technical for the busy trainer/evaluator, they have been included for three reasons. Firstly, there is an unfortunate tendency for people to assume that evaluation data can be collected only through questionnaires administered at the end of courses and backed up by the odd interview. This review, although by no means exhaustive, is intended to demonstrate that there are many ways of gathering useful data from a wide range of sources. Secondly, much data can be gathered in these ways with very little effort or cost. As much as anything it is a matter of taking advantage of observations and recordings that already exist, but it is also important to ensure that

STAKEHOLDERS / FOCUSES	A PARTICIPANTS ON COURSE Beginning + Midway	B EX-COURSE PARTICIPANTS	C BOSSES

1 OBJECTIVES CONTEXT	• Career history aims
	• Learning objectives
	• Experience of reward system + role of course
	• Experience of company culture
	• Changes in learning objectives
			• Learning objectives
			  – general
			  – specific
			• Role of course

2 PROCESSES	• Course elements: most/least useful. Why? • Culture of prog? • Changes would make and how? • Changes made and how? • Length of course		• What should be improved? Why? • Length of course
3 INPUTS	• Perspective from different workshops • Quality of lectures, tutors, methods • Content?		?
4 ADMIN	• Info about prog's existence? • How were they selected – procedure? • Domestics – hotel, info received, communication?		• Input and role in selection procedure
5 OUTCOMES	MIDWAY – Overall Value + 2 specific examples of application at work • Career progress, present and possible future • Hindrance in achieving/using it • Networking?		Overall value + 2 specific examples • Career progress, present and possible future • Appraisal data. To what extent +ve and –ve as result of course

Figure 4.6   Draft data matrix according to stakeholders and focuses

the processes of selection and recording are carried out with a little more rigour and without undue bias.

Finally, let me reiterate that while many of these approaches may be quite valuable, it is best to use them in combination with other media

D TRAINING PROVIDERS (LOUGHBOROUGH)	E TRAINING CLIENTS (FORD)	F SENIOR MANAGERS
• Want from evaluation? • Learning objectives • Context of course • Fits in with dept and staffing? • How prog run and supported • Perception of Ford objectives	• Want from evaluation? • Learning objectives • Perception of Loughborough objectives • Context of course • Fits in with culture?	• Reasons for funding prog • Criteria for success • Model of ideal manager • Culture, current and ideal • Course as vehicle for change? • Sub aims—networking?
• What worked well/less well? Why? • Possible changes and how? • How has course evolved? Culture?		Any contact?
• Staffing and decisions on content and why? • Key elements of content • Links with participants outside workshop	• Contact with tutors • Perspectives of key elements of content	Any contact?
• Links with other organization Communication, planning, info, etc • Problem areas, past and present		?
• Follow-up? Evaluation? If so, results? • Anecdotal re outcomes/ value	• Follow-up? If so, results? • Anecdotal re outcomes/ value • List of participants and turnover	• Overall value/ impressions • Any evidence • Sources

Figure 4.6 concluded

and methods. Each provides an impression that is partial, and people interested in constructing a reasonable likeness of the 'truth' should always be looking for impressions from different perspectives.

5   Data collection methods

Although many people may feel that methods are the key part of any evaluation activity, the message that has been repeated several times in the book up to this point is that there are many other aspects of evaluation each of which may be at least as important as measures and data collection techniques. This message is reinforced by astute practitioners such as Patton (1981), Hamblin (1974), and Guba and Lincoln (1989) who are most emphatic that techniques should not be seen as ends in themselves.

The most common way of classifying methods in the last few years has been according to whether they are essentially quantitative or qualitative. The distinction is again akin to the *scientific-constructivist* dimensions of approaches to evaluation discussed earlier, and it is therefore assumed that no immediate elaboration of these terms is needed.

My initial attempt at classifying the various methods used this dimension. But it turned out to be rather difficult to locate methods in any absolute sense, since there seemed to be distinctions between the essence of a technique, and how it could be used in practice. For example, a learning style questionnaire (LSQ) (Honey and Mumford, 1982) or a questionnaire on values (Hofstede, 1980) are essentially *quantitative* data collection methods. Responses are immediately recorded in the form of numbers: this is the essence of these techniques, and the process of recording cannot be changed without invalidating the whole questionnaire. But the LSQ can be used to do research on how students learn, or to help managers understand their own learning process, or as a basis for assigning course participants to groups, and so on. There is a similar contrast in the case of an 'open interview', where the data are essentially *qualitative* (i.e. words spoken by interviewer and interviewee), but interviews may vary greatly in the amount of influence that the interviewee will have on the kind of words that are recorded, and the analysis of the interview may also vary from an open ended review by interviewer and interviewee to a tightly coded (and quantitative) analysis of the transcript conducted by an independent observer.

One key issue that begins to emerge from these examples is the extent to which the subject is able to influence the way the data are collected (rather than simply responding along predetermined channels). With some methods there is considerable flexibility and the preferred way can be worked out jointly by evaluator and subject. With others the methods are clearly defined and they leave no room for negotiation: the evaluator chooses the method and the subject either responds appropriately, or declines to participate.

This question about the opportunities for control and flexibility that are inherent in different research methods is an important feature of Torbert's (1981) critique of so much of current educational research. His main argument is that educational research has been spectacularly incapable of providing clear answers to questions simply because it has always emphasized unilateral control by the researchers, and it has rarely considered that the subjects of this research could, or should, have much influence on how the research is to be done – let alone play a part in the interpretation of results. The answer proposed is to consider the subject as a co-researcher who is able to participate and share insights with the researcher – and this is a theme that is taken up by a number of others such as Reason and Rowan (1981).

The question of *control* forms another aspect of the *scientific-constructivist* dimension. In view of the importance of control in understanding the *use* of data collection methods I have decided to use it as the main way of classifying methods in this chapter. The techniques and methods in Figure 5.1 are therefore located in this dimension initially according to where the *essence* of the technique, as it is generally understood, would place it, and then a possible range of variation according to *use* is indicated by arrows on either side. The ten techniques or methods were chosen for two main reasons: either because they are commonly used, well known (and occasionally misunderstood); or because they are less well known but have considerable utility in the kind of circumstances likely to be encountered by evaluators. They vary considerably in breadth; some being straightforward techniques for use in particular circumstances, others being general methods which may be used in many different ways in a multiplicity of circumstances. They will be discussed in the order given in Figure 5.1.

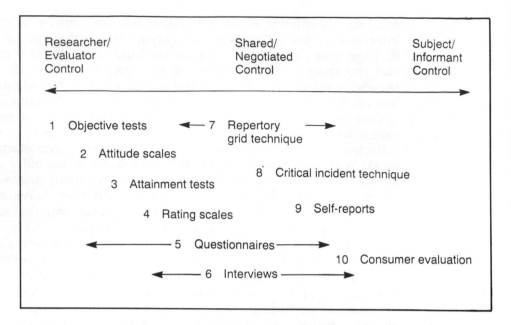

Figure 5.1 Location of common data collection techniques and methods on the dimension of control

Objective tests

These are sometimes known as personality tests, with examples such as the Myers-Briggs and 16-PF being frequently used in personnel work. What is distinctive about most 'objective' tests is that they are constructed mathematically by looking for patterns in response to large numbers of questions answered by hundreds of people. Questions that tend to be answered in similar ways are grouped together to form scales which are given labels – sometimes using everyday terms such as *anxious-stable*, sometimes using invented terms such as *sizothymia-clotothymia*. The justification for using nonsense words like the latter is that since the scale is constructed 'objectively', scores on it are unlikely to have a precise meaning in everyday language, and one should therefore avoid confusing people with everyday labels.

Most objective tests involve a list of questions and the subject is invited to make simple responses to each one, such as answering *yes* or *no*. For example:

1 Do you prefer action to planning?	Yes	No
2 Would you rate yourself as energetic?	Yes	No
3 Would you be unhappy if you were prevented from meeting any new people?	Yes	No
4 Are you bothered by what others think of you?	Yes	No
5 Do you wait for others to speak before you speak?	Yes	No

These questions have been adapted from two widely used personality tests. Positive answers to the first three are seen as signs of *extroversion*; positive answers to the latter two indicate a tendency to avoid confrontations (*denial*).

Because of the construction of these scales and the fact that the form of response is totally prescribed (if any questions are missed out or not answered in the approved manner this usually invalidates the whole test), there is very little opportunity for the informant to influence the form of the test. Indeed this is one of the main aims in the construction and administration of such tests.

There are also examples of tests which are essentially 'objective', but which are based on qualitative data (which is not in any way predetermined). The best known example of this is the Thematic Apperception Test (TAT) which uses stories written by people about what they think is taking place in an incident depicted in a drawing or photograph. This is one of the techniques used in diagnosing managerial competencies (Boyatsis, 1982), and the growing popularity of this approach is likely to result in widespread application of the TAT. Despite seeming open-ended and qualitative, it is however a tightly controlled test. Protocols for analysis of TAT stories are very carefully prescribed and are carried out by expert analysis; moreover the subject should not normally know what it is that the tester is looking for.

Another feature of objective tests which should be understood well by those contemplating using them for evaluation purposes is that they assume that an individual's personality is a fixed trait and does not change over time. It is therefore taken as a sign of a good test if it produces very similar results when administered on two different occasions to the same sample of individuals. Hence an attempt to administer a personality test to participants before and after a management course should, in theory, indicate no changes however good the course has been in other respects – and any evidence of changes in test results might be indicative of a weak test, rather than a strong course.

The main use of these tests for evaluators should be in the early diagnostic stages when the focus is upon *context*. Some knowledge of personality traits may be of help in selecting managers for particular forms of training or development, particularly when there is a clear link between the two (for example, TATs measuring achievement motivation may be used to select high flyers or potential recruits for new business ventures). And the education system has made extensive use of intelligence tests in its selection procedures (i.e. the 11+ Test as a criterion for admission to all Grammar Schools in the UK until the late 1970s, or the Graduate Management Admissions Test (GMAT) as a major determinant of admissions to graduate Business Schools around the world).

Objective tests clearly have their function, by they do require large scale operations to make them worthwhile – unless appropriate standards and norms have been developed in advance it can be very difficult to interpret individual results. They should normally be used only by (or under the supervision of) someone who has been trained in their use since they represent an advanced and complex technology; but for those who still wish to try their hands, not all tests are restricted to psychologists and many books exist for guidance both at the popular and technical ends of the markets. (Eysenck and Eysenck, 1967 and Buros, 1978, perhaps representing two of these extremes.)

Attitude scales

Attitude scales are less 'technical' than objective tests, but they still represent a very extensive area of study. For example, as far back as 1937, Allport identified forty-seven different ways in which the concept of 'attitude' has been defined (Allport, 1937). A slightly more recent definition is that of Krech, Crutchfield and Ballachey (1962, p. 146):

> An attitude can be defined as an enduring system of three components centering about a single object: the beliefs about the object – the *cognitive component*; the affect connected with the object – the *feeling component*; and the disposition to take action with respect to the object – the *action tendency component*.

Thus, to take a simple example from evaluation, it might be decided to measure attitudes towards 'delegation' before and after a human relations training course for managers. These three components could be measured by the questions in Figure 5.2 (where respondents are asked to ring the number which best represents their view on the continuum that is assumed to exist between the two extreme statements).

1	Most junior managers here do not have the ability to take greater responsibility.	1 2 3 4 5 6 7	Most junior managers here are quite capable of taking on more responsibility.
2	I am uneasy giving responsibility to subordinates in areas for which I am accountable.	1 2 3 4 5 6 7	I am quite happy giving genuine responsibility to my subordinates.
3	I would usually encourage junior managers who show willingness to take additional responsibility.	1 2 3 4 5 6 7	I would not usually welcome suggestions from junior managers that they might take on more responsibility.

Figure 5.2 Attitude scales measuring cognitive, feeling, and action tendency components

It will be noticed that the 'good' end of the scale (if you are in favour of delegation) is at the right-hand end and will be indicated by high scores on the first two questions; but on the third question it is at the left-hand end and will be indicated by low scores. This simple device of reversing the direction and scores of positive responses is intended to force the subject to think about each question independently, thus reducing the chance of 'response set bias' where the subject decides which end is the good end after completing two or three questions and simply marks all the remaining questions at the same end of the scale.

The form of scale used in the example is known as a 'semantic differential' scale; the main feature being a pair of opposite (or contrasting) words or phrases which are placed on opposite sides of the page with a string of numbers between them. The respondent is then invited to indicate his or her view by ringing a number (or marking a point on a scale placed underneath these numbers) indicating a position or view somewhere between the two stated extremes. There are two other forms of scale which are frequently used to measure attitudes: Likert and Thurstone scales. Both are named after their inventors.

Using these two scales respectively the first question in the above example might be rewritten:

Likert	Strongly agree	Agree	Disagree	Strongly disagree
The average junior manager here does not have the ability to take greater responsibility.	1	2	3	4

Thurstone

Most junior managers here do not have the ability to take on more responsibility	Most junior managers could take on a little more responsibility	Most junior managers are quite capable of taking on more responsibility
1	2	3

These last two examples provide four and three response categories respectively. A lot has been written about the ideal number of response categories to offer in attitude questionnaires – and whether or not to avoid central categories. My own preference is to use as few categories as possible: anything above seven points in the scale seems to give a spurious impression of accuracy. Central response categories do not seem to be a problem with scales of seven points, but in those with fewer points it is often preferable to use an even number of points thus forcing the respondent to make a decision one way or another. My own preferences are for four or seven point scales.

Attitude measures are still used quite frequently to evaluate general management courses, and they were also used extensively by Hogarth (1979) in the evaluation of the CEDEP programme at INSEAD in France.

In contrast to personality tests they have an obvious application in the measurement of individual and group changes over a period of time, and they may be focused on a wide range of things – such as relationships, management styles, other individuals, conditions of work, the management course, the organization itself, and so on. It should also be recognized that they fall near the 'scientific' end of the methodological dimension. As such it is assumed that attitudes 'exist' within people, and the job of the researcher or evaluator is to measure the strength of these attitudes, normally without the respondent being aware of what is being measured. Indeed it remains important that the subject has minimal influence upon the process of attitude measurement – other than responding in the appropriate manner.

There are no standards about the ideal number of questions to use in measuring an attitude. A number of considerations need to be balanced against each other: on one hand a large number of questions should provide many perspectives on the attitude to be measured without making it too obvious what is being investigated; on the other hand long questionnaires are tedious to complete (and analyse) and the number of questions may spread too far to provide accurate measurement of any single attitude. In practice such questionnaires vary from one to several hundred questions. My compromise length is in the range of six to twelve questions. As with any quantitative measure, interpretation can cause difficulties until a bank of data has been built up from previous occasions. But attitude measures do have an initial advantage over objective tests, since a change in scores between two administrations in the former case may indicate that the attitude has gone up or down, while in the latter case it indicates merely that you have a poor test!

Finally there is no reason why evaluators should not have a go at making up their own attitude scales, particularly if they are to be used as supplementary evidence (whether for *proving, improving, learning or controlling*). Clarity of construction is essential (the examples I have given above in this section are perhaps a little wordy). The usual strictures about avoiding asking double questions in a single item, and about avoiding double negatives in the wording, apply as ever. For those wishing to pursue these methods more seriously Oppenheim (1966) remains one of the most useful texts.

Attainment tests

Attainment tests focus almost exclusively on the *outcomes* from management training, education and development. Depending on the context, such tests might concentrate on assessing levels of knowledge, skills, or comprehension.

Starting with the first of these, most tests of knowledge *per se* are intended to provide an unambiguous assessment – which means constructing tests that have clearly identified right and wrong answers. It is also assumed that the course or programme to be evaluated has reasonably clear objectives against which the assessment questions can be formulated.

Perhaps the most common form of 'objective' attainment test is the multiple choice format. Thus on an international management course participants might be asked to answer a list of twenty-five questions including the one shown in Figure 5.3.

Question 6

The North-South dialogue was: (*ring one number*):

(a)	A satellite-based information system linking the two hemispheres.	1
(b)	The process of determining regional aid finance in the UK on an annual basis.	2
(c)	A series of discussions between leaders of developed and undeveloped countries about the future of the world's economy.	3
(d)	The historic talks aimed at avoiding the US Civil War, commemorated annually by peace campaigners.	4

Figure 5.3 A multiple choice 'knowledge' question

Although multiple-choice questions give the appearance of objectivity (they can be scored by computer, and are being increasingly used in interactive computer-based learning), they are quite difficult to construct particularly if they cover complex concepts. One of the major difficulties is in making the wrong answers look as plausible as the right answer (perhaps the reader could try inventing a more plausible set of 'wrong' answers for the North-South dialogue question). Another problem is that when using such questions on a before-and-after basis participants will be alerted on the initial occasion and will be sensitive during the course to any information relating to these questions. The resulting increase in scores on test items may not be representative of their learning across the course.

The last issue is a problem if one wishes to use objective attainment tests (such as those based on multiple choice questions) for purposes of *proving*; but it may be a positive asset if the evaluation is intended to contribute to *learning*. Warr, Bird and Rackham (1970) claim, based on experiments conducted with supervisors attending accident prevention courses, that pre-tests of knowledge will increase performance on knowledge tests after the course, even when items in the latter were not contained in the former. Thus pre-tests on specific items can apparently lead to greater knowledge gains in general in such a course. Unfortunately these authors do not attempt to explain *why* this should be so; but that is another limitation of 'scientific' evaluation designs.

Apart from multiple-choice questions there are a number of other types of question which can be included in objective attainment tests. For example, a list of statements about the subject matter of the course is presented and the participant is invited to indicate whether they are true or false; or the participant can be asked to match one group of words with another. Thus in the example of self-assessments of knowledge given in the following section (see Figure 5.8), the graduate engineers were asked to indicate from a long list of company functions (including production, personnel, R & D, accounts and purchasing) in which function the particular terminology (invoice, lead time, tolerance limits, buffer, budgetary control) would most likely be encountered.

One of the criticisms of objective tests is that they concentrate on 'rote' learning, and cannot indicate whether the subject has actually *understood* what he or she is supposed to have learnt. Tests of understanding and comprehension generally require more open-ended questions (which normally means that scoring is a more subjective process). An example of a partially open-ended question also comes from the evaluation of an extended induction course for graduate recruits to an engineering company (see p. 91).

Provided that the students had not been given a model answer to this question in their lecture notes (and this was unlikely since the evaluators and lecturers were kept apart during this study) the answers to this little problem would indicate something of their understanding of production layout. This is the essence of the examination process where students who have been given information in one form are expected to be able to reorganize the material in order to provide coherent answers to questions that are similar to, but different from,

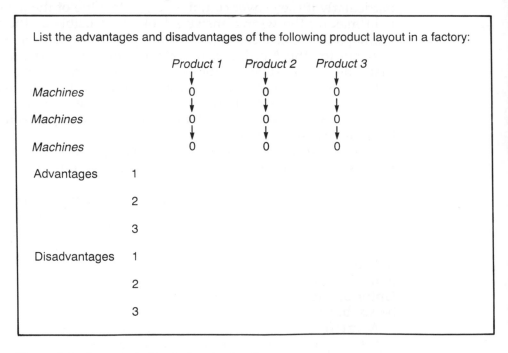

Figure 5.4   Open-ended test of understanding

questions they have encountered before – and it indicates the kind of learning that Pask and Scott (1972) label as 'holist' (as opposed to 'serialist') learning.

The assessment of exams and other more complex pieces of work, such as essays and projects, is often criticized as being highly subjective. My own experience of this is that it is possible for examiners independently to achieve a high degree of correlation between their assessments, provided they are in agreement about the criteria of value to be applied. Within a traditional framework of values the following criteria might apply in ascending order in assessing academic essays or exams:

5 Deals elegantly with the question; also produces new synthesis, ideas or concepts.
4 Constructs a sound argument backed by a reasonable amount of data.
3 Gets most of the facts right, but does not build much of an argument with them.
2 Able to recall a few facts correctly; but they relate only vaguely to the question.
1 Does not seem to know much at all of relevance to the question.

In the case of a university degree, Category 2 would normally be on the borderline between a fail and a pass, and Category 1 would be a certain fail; the other categories would indicate ascending levels of pass marks.

This is also quite similar to some of the older performance appraisal rating scales, which were so neatly parodied in *The Sunday Times* in 1971 as shown in Figure 5.5.

Communication skills	Talks to God	1
	Talks to the Angels	2
	Talks to himself	3
	Argues with himself	4
	Loses those arguments	5
Agility	Clears tall buildings with a single leap	1
	Needs a run before leaping	2
	Clears low buildings	3
	Crashes into buildings	4
	Cannot recognize a building	5

Figure 5.5 Rating scales for performance appraisal (from *The Sunday Times*, 1971)

Returning to the problem of assessing examination answers; this is not too difficult with traditional knowledge-based questions. But the problem becomes much greater if unconventional criteria are included – such as creativity. What if a student produces in answer to a question about the state of industrial relations in the UK, an insightful cartoon?

How is that to be weighed against the model essay which outlines the main forces at work in the industrial relations scene, and sets these neatly within an historical context? Another kind of problem arises when project reports are to be assessed as part of an action learning programme. What relative credit should be given to (a) the quality of what the student has done during the period of the project, versus (b) the quality of the student's written account of what he or she did during the project? Even with cases such as these I have noticed a remarkable convergence in the marks awarded independently by examiners working in the same departments or institutions – which seems to imply the evolution of shared implicit value systems amongst colleagues over a period of time. Naturally, their students are still expected to grasp these value systems within a rather shorter period of time – but that is merely part of the academic 'game'!

Tests of skill attainment are rather rare in educational settings, but more common on management and supervisory training courses. They normally involve observations of participants performing an activity which simulates what they would be required to do at work – chairing a meeting, holding a disciplinary interview, participating in a problem-solving meeting, etc. These were discussed above under the general heading of 'observation' as a medium for data collection; the main issue being whether the observers should, or should not, impose predetermined frameworks on their observations. In the case of attainment tests it is generally necessary to have some framework or template against which observations can be compared in order to determine the level of performance.

The framework of excellence against which the skilled performance is to be measured will itself be a matter of opinion, even if that opinion comes from 'experts' in the field. Furthermore, the recognition of expertize may vary with perspective. In the case of assessing the teaching skills of students or lecturers there are two perspectives which are clearly distinct: that of the expert lecturer, and that of the expert learner. The behaviours that fit perfectly with the lecturer's model of good teaching may be quite inappropriate for helping the student learn; and the student's view of a good lecturer may have little to do with a good 'performance'. My own preference is to emphasize the learner's perspective, and I encourage lecturers to do likewise.

Self and peer assessment also have possibilities here, particularly when each student takes it in turn to run a 'session' while the remainder provide the audience. Such assessments might thus be seen as being some way between the teacher's and learner's perspectives. For example, variations of self and peer assessment have been used for some time on postgraduate courses at Lancaster University, and one example comes from part of the formal assessment for a small group of students on a diploma course for whom I was the tutor. Each student rated his or her own contribution, and those of all other students in the group on a scale ranging from A to E. We had discussed for about an hour what each of these grades should mean, with the assumption that E would imply a 'fail' and A 'distinction'.

The assessments were conducted in confidence, and were collected by myself. The average of all the grades given to each student then counted directly towards his or her final assessment for the diploma. The grades awarded to each of these students by themselves and others (including myself) are listed in Figure 5.6.

		Assessment of:				
	Student No.	1	2	3	4	5
Assessed by	1	B	B	B−	B	C+
	2	B−	B+	B−	C+	C+
	3	C	C+	B	B	B−
	4	B−	B−	B	B	B+
	5	C+	B−	B−	B	B
	Tutor	C+	B−	B−	B	B−
	Result	C+	B−	B−	B	B−

Figure 5.6 Self, peer and tutor assessment of teaching skills

Two points interested me about these results. Firstly there was quite a high degree of agreement between all the observers with regard to the quality of each contribution; and secondly, most of the self assessments were slightly higher than the average of assessments made by others, but not excessively so. Statisticians will no doubt point to the small sample size and the small variance in the ratings; but I found this result encouraging, and I think that the multiple perspectives that can be brought to bear in self and peer assessments of skills still have a lot to recommend them. The students may even learn a little from the process of doing this, too.

With the exception of the last example, assessments are generally controlled quite strongly by the evaluator (or examiner) – and even in the last example I reserved the right to adjust the final marks if I felt that justice had not been done (although I didn't use this right). When assessment of individuals is being used as a way of evaluating the course or programme through which they are passing then it is likely to be aimed at *proving*, and if the assessments are collated centrally from a large number of courses or institutions then it is almost certain that they will be used to *control* standards. On occasions when intermediate assessments are made during a course (as with programmed learning or mid-course essays), these ought to contribute to the individual's *learning*, if the feedback is managed appropriately. In theory such assessments could be used to *improve* the course as it is happening, or afterwards, but I have not yet encountered any examples of this happening in practice.

When assessments are being used to inform decisions about individuals it is important that they are well validated and reliable. This is not quite so important when the results are being used to inform decisions about courses and programmes since averaging of results will reduce the range of error, and the decisions themselves may have less drastic human implications (although the closure of a department, college or university determined partly by assessment-type data would obviously have very profound effects). Apart from the general importance of accuracy, the classic critique of assessments is that they are normally linked to selection procedures. Individuals may be selected for jobs, for certification (degrees, diplomas, etc.), or for admission to education establishments. But in order for the assessments to have any credibility, or use, they must distinguish between those who 'pass' and those who 'fail'. Within hierarchical educational systems, or organizations, the opportunities for reaching the top are very limited, and therefore the majority of people must be labelled as 'failures' at some stage. This may be particularly bad in school systems where some children are perpetually labelled as failures, and it is, of course, a major justification for non-selective schooling in the UK. However, when certifications and selections are to be made there is little alternative to assessment, and in these cases it is worth remembering the limitations and problems inherent in this approach.

Rating scales

Whereas attitude scales can be quite complex to construct and interpret, rating scales are very straightforward and extremely flexible. For this reason they are widely used in end-of-course questionnaires, and often form the basis for monitoring and controlling tutor performance within institutions. Most rating scales take the form of one of the attitude scales illustrated in the previous section, the main difference being that they employ only one question for each object: hence the greater simplicity.

The questionnaire illustrated in Chapter 3 (Figure 3.3) contains in Question 4 a series of rating scales about the usefulness of different activities on the course. The important aspect in interpreting the results of such scales is to make comparisons internally: were the 'formal lectures' seen as more, or less, useful than the 'role play exercises', and so on. This form of analysis should tell the evaluator where the problems lie, and what should be investigated further; unfortunately it does not give much indication of what might be done to solve the problems (other than to remove the offending activities altogether). But this of course is a more general problem with 'scientific' evaluation methods.

Rating scales can be, and are, constructed with ease to examine responses to any of the five focuses discussed in Chapter 3: context, administration, inputs, process, and outcomes. But before moving on it is worth looking at a frequently used form of rating scale which often covers the last three: the session assessment form. The example in

Figure 5.7 contains six questions based on semantic differential scales, with two questions covering each of these focuses.

The last session was:		
1 Badly prepared	1 2 3 4 5 6 7	Well prepared
2 Relevant to my work	1 2 3 4 5 6 7	Irrelevant to my work
In the last session:		
3 Discussion was constructive	1 2 3 4 5 6 7	Discussion was not constructive
4 I played an active role	1 2 3 4 5 6 7	I took a back seat
5 I learnt a lot	1 2 3 4 5 6 7	I learnt very little
6 There is much that I intend to make use of	1 2 3 4 5 6 7	There is nothing I can use

Figure 5.7 Session assessment rating scales focusing on input, process, and outcome aspects

One further example of rating scales involves their use to assess the learning or development of individuals resulting from training or education. The questionnaire from which the items in Figure 5.8 were selected was administered to a group of engineering graduates before and after participating in an extended induction course in an engineering company: it was a summative evaluation intended to demonstrate the value of this kind of project-based course (see Easterby-Smith, Krishna and Ashton, 1977 for further details). The change in ratings on this question was linked to a number of more 'objective' indicators of learning (all used on a before-and-after basis), which were discussed under the general heading of 'attainment tests' in the previous section. It is a moot point whether such self-assessment should be trusted. In the example above we found a negative correlation between changes in these questions and more objective indicators. Thus the graduates apparently *overestimated* their increased knowledge on the second application of the questionnaire. This may be compared with Burgoyne's (1973a) finding that managers attending a course *reduced* their ratings

To what extent are you familiar with the following terminology? (Ring one number on each line):					
	Very little extent	**Little extent**	**Some extent**	**Quite a lot**	**Great extent**
Invoice	1	2	3	4	5
Lead time	1	2	3	4	5
Tolerance limits	1	2	3	4	4
Buffer	1	2	3	4	5
Budgetary control	1	2	3	4	5

Figure 5.8 Self-ratings of student learning

of their initial knowledge as the course progressed, presumably as their awareness of their own ignorance increased.

Uncertainties such as these about the proper interpretation of rating scales do not prove the case for keeping the subject (or informant) in the dark, and for devising measures that are proof from tampering and interference. But they do provide a cautionary note about reading too much significance into the results of rating scales. They should be regarded as a 'low technology' way of getting quantitative evaluation data which can signal to trainers, participants and stakeholders what may be taking place; they are, however, of dubious accuracy, and the evaluator who is concerned about quantitative accuracy should regard them merely as diagnostic supplements to a more extensive bag of tricks.

Questionnaires

In some respects 'questionnaires' are a whole methodology on their own: that is a class of methods rather than any single method. And therefore it is not surprising to find them covering a wide range on the dimension between full evaluator control and full informant control. Nevertheless, given that questionnaires allow quite a lot of latitude both in formulation and response, they have been located in Figure 5.1 somewhat to the right of the various tests and attitude/rating scales.

The sample end-of-course questionnaire illustrated in Chapter 3 (Figure 3.3), was written deliberately to illustrate a range of question types that might be used in such questionnaires. The most important distinction to understand is that between 'closed questions' and 'open questions'. Closed questions are constructed specifically to limit the number of possible answers that the respondent might give so that this will facilitate collation of responses from different individuals (often with the help of a computer which will both read and score the responses). Open questions point the respondent in a general direction without prescribing the nature and form of response that is acceptable. Question 5 from Figure 3.3 is reproduced below as an example of an open question:

5   What specific changes would you suggest to this course in order to enhance its effectiveness?

If this question was to be re-written as a closed question it might take the following form:

5   This course could be made more effective if it was:

Longer	1	2	3	Shorter
Faster pace	1	2	3	Slower pace
More academic	1	2	3	More practical
More related to				Less related to
the industry	1	2	3	the industry
Etc.				

The obvious drawback with closed questions, particularly when informants are being asked to think ahead and use some imagination, is that most of the questions may be getting at things which the informant does not think are important. Thus a large number of closed questions might be required to get at the one suggestion which the informant could offer in a single sentence within an open question. This also points to the need for questionnaires which employ closed questions to be pre-tested in order to reduce the amount of redundant information that they produce. Whatever the form of questions employed within questionnaires it should be remembered that they are based primarily on one-way communication: it is not normally open for the informant to clarify or argue with the questions posed. He or she can either respond as requested, or fail to return the questionnaire. Even the ultimate in open questions, 'Is there anything else that you would like to say?' does not really solve this problem, because the evaluator is then unable to clarify or probe further into the cryptic remarks that may be produced in response to this question.

The main strength of questionnaires is that they can be used to gather data from a large number of people without much cost. They may also be valuable when used in conjunction with other methods; for example, to provide an initial screening to see which particular informant could most beneficially be interviewed.

There are, of course, many limitations to questionnaires: they are more useful for gathering superficial data than 'in depth' data; they cannot adapt easily to changing circumstances and needs; and the response rates to questionnaires can be extremely low, particularly when distributed by mail.

The design and use of questionnaires is an extremely complex area, and it will not be possible to do proper justice to it in this book, and for those who wish to take the matter further Oppenheim (1966) is again recommended. From my pragmatic viewpoint there is little to be lost in experimenting with the use of questionnaires, although it is always worth trying them out on three or four friends before progressing to any wider application. It is worth using a range of question types to provide some triangulation, although too many changes in question type within one questionnaire may be rather demanding on the poor respondent. There are many strictures about what to do and what to avoid in the wording of questions, and the formulation of questionnaires, but although it is quite easy to be *aware* of these things, they can be quite hard to put into practice. I now find it rather easier to construct 'bad' questionnaires than 'good' questionnaires and Figure 5.9 provides an illustration of the former with some examples of features that are all too common in questionnaires.

The following questionnaire is intended to obtain your views about the construction of questionnaires.

1   What are your views on questions that are worded rather vaguely?

2   Please indicate whether you think 'double questions' provide economy of scale or are useful in forcing the respondent to think hard.
Yes   ☐   No   ☐

3   Do you agree with us that 'leading questions' are undesirable and should be avoided whenever possible?
Yes   ☐   No   ☐

4   'Double negatives' are not a good thing to remove from draft questionnaires whenever possible.
Yes   ☐   No   ☐

5   If answer categories are provided it is important that they are (please tick one):
Drawn from similar categories   ☐

Appropriate to the question   ☐

Agree   ☐

Disagree   ☐

6   The above items were 'warm-up questions' and will not be included in the analysis; our main purpose in this questionnaire is to find out how many extra-marital affairs you have had:
More than 10   ☐

5–9   ☐

2–4   ☐

1   ☐

None   ☐

Not married   ☐

Figure 5.9   An awful questionnaire mainly about questionnaires

Interviews

With interviews comes the possibility of two-way communication when gathering evaluation data. They therefore have greater potential than the methods discussed above for allowing the informant to influence the process of data collection. As with questionnaires, there are many approaches that may be adopted in evaluation interviews, and Figure 5.10 lists some of the general alternatives. It should be appreciated that 'closed' and 'structured' approaches to interviewing maintain greater control for the evaluator; while 'open' and 'shared' approaches to interviewing allow for more control from the informant.

Type of interview	Characteristics
1 Closed	Responses required within predetermined answer categories.
2 Structured	Interviewer questions are predetermined, but answers are not restricted.
3 Open	A general guide or checklist of questions is normally followed, but there is flexibility about what is targeted.
4 Shared	The evaluator's problems/questions are shared with the respondent, and these are explored in whatever way seems appropriate.

Figure 5.10 Types of interview for evaluation purposes

Closed interviews

Closed interviews, as defined above, are rather like verbal structured questionnaires. Since they are based essentially upon one-way communication, they share much of the disadvantages of these: it takes numerous questions to yield much data, and it also may be rather difficult to make sense of the data that has been yielded. The one advantage which is not insignificant is that they ensure some response (providing the informant does not refuse to co-operate), and for this reason closed interviews are frequently used in market and political research when information is to be solicited from strangers. I have used closed interviews on a couple of occasions in evaluation studies, and I found myself rather embarrassed by the lack of information yielded by them. Furthermore, since the information is frequently quantified (as when respondents are asked to indicate which of a number of multiple responses printed on a card they agree with), the sample sizes typically found in evaluation studies rarely allow any sense to be made of these results at all.

Structured interviews

Structured interviews are rather similar to open-ended questionnaires. The interviewer is expected to read out the question precisely as worded on the interview sheet, and the answer is then recorded on audio tape or/and in note form by the interviewer. It is then up to the interviewer to probe and enquire in more depth regarding the answers to particular questions if this seems appropriate. The format allows for a higher degree of standardization, and for some flexibility and exchange between the interviewer and the informant. For the first time the questions asked by the evaluator are being influenced by the answers provided by the informant. But because there is not much flexibility in the structure of the interview it is important that the evaluator has a good idea of what he or she is looking for at the outset, and is therefore able to provide a reason for the questions asked. This means that structured interviews are often most appropriate when focusing on a particular area of a course (such as the outcomes), and they may also adopt a particular technique (such as the critical incident technique, discussed below). In the case of management training courses where participants disperse to different parts of the country or subsequently the world even, a further advantage is that such interviews may be conducted by different individuals who have no prior contact with each other – and the results thus produced are likely to be reasonably consistent.

Open interviews

Open interviews normally employ a general guide or checklist of questions which can be embellished as the evaluator thinks fit. Provided the list of questions is not too long, it is often possible to conduct most of the interview without reference to the checklist – until the end when it is necessary to ensure that most of the specified areas have been covered. Thus open interviews can easily be conducted in very informal settings such as pubs, on trains, and so on. Their main strength is in opening up questions of importance and in covering a wide range of possible areas while leaving open the possibility of deeper investigation into areas that look problematic. Thus an open interview might even use the five focuses described in Chapter 3 as general areas for discussion without any more narrowing of issues at an initial stage. And they may be used to investigate any aspect of training and developmental programmes, whether they are being reviewed afterwards, or evaluated while they are in progress.

Shared interviews

Shared interviews take a further step towards allowing greater control to the informant. They are similar to what Massarik calls 'the phenomenal interview':

> This interview is characterised by maximal mutuality of trust obtaining a genuine and deeply experienced caring between interviewer and interviewee, and a commitment to joint search for shared understanding.
>
> (Massarik, 1981, p. 203.)

In other words it involves both interviewer and informant sharing their ideas, observations, and interests about, say, what is taking place during a management course; and over several conversations they may come to a better understanding of what this is. The difference in role between the evaluator and the informants (as colleagues or participants), is simply that the evaluator's interest may be a continuing obsession whereas the informant's interest may be no more than a passing concern.

Depth interviews

There is another form of interview which is occasionally discussed as a distinct type, but for our purposes I would locate it as either 'shared', or midway between that and 'open' interviews. This is the 'depth' interview (Ruddock, 1981, p. 63), in which 'the subject is asked to follow and verbalize his own train of thought, without guidance'. It requires handling by interviewers who are skilled as counsellors or psychotherapists since this kind of interview often gets into sensitive personal areas of anxiety, denial, obsession, or whatever. Such depth interviews may be very useful in identifying fundamental problems about the operation of educational programmes (as when a particular form of examination system is causing great anxiety amongst students which manifests itself in laziness or over-indulgence in drink). But apart from the obvious need for a highly-skilled interviewer, it may be an extremely time-consuming approach; furthermore the cynic would claim that it is not unlikely for an approach which involves looking for symptoms of anxiety and defensiveness to come up with answers and solutions in like vein.

Advice to interviewers

Patton gives some words of advice for those who are involved in 'qualitative' interviewing. The fundamental principle of this form of interviewing is, as he says 'to provide a framework within which respondents can express their own understandings in their own terms' (Patton, 1980, p. 205). These correspond roughly to what I have called 'structured' and 'open' interviews, since both of these involve the collection of qualitative data; and, in addition, these are where the interaction between the interviewer and the interviewee is most demanding. Firstly, as with questionnaires the usual strictures apply here about clarity of questions, and about not phrasing them in such a way that they indicate the desirable answer (leading questions).

Secondly, Patton is quite concerned about the use of time within an interview, and stresses the importance of maintaining control on the side of the interviewer (which rather betrays his position on the control dimension!). Patton lists three suggestions to help the interviewer maintain control:

1   knowing what one wants to find out;
2   asking the right questions to get the desired answers; and

3   giving appropriate verbal and non-verbal feedback to the person
being interviewed.

(Patton, 1980, p. 243.)

A third piece of advice is the importance of phrasing questions in
such a way that they encourage the informant to open up, rather than
simply answering 'yes' or 'no'. Examples of such questions are:

• Is the course going well at the moment?
• Did you learn much from your MBA?
• Was the counselling interview of any use?

The problem with questions like these is that they not only provoke
a somewhat symbolic response, but they also set up a pattern in the
sequence of questions from which it is very hard to break out into more
open forms. They can also make the interview seem more like a quiz
or interrogation, which once again discourages the informant from
opening up in any way. In order to have provided more fruitful information these three questions might have been rephrased as follows:

• How is the course going . . . what do you like most/least about it?
• Could you tell me something about one or two most important
things you learnt from your MBA?
• In what ways (if any) do you think that the counselling interview
will be of use to you in your work?

Patton's fourth piece of advice, which I find interesting, is the notion
of presuppositions that can be incorporated into questions asked during
an interview. In essence these questions assume as a starting point that
some kind of change or learning has actually taken place, and in some
senses they are 'leading' questions. ('When did you stop beating your
wife?' is a classic example of a presupposition question.) Of the three
rephrased questions given above, the first contains the presupposition
that the informant did have some feelings about the course, the second
that she or he would be able to identify things that had been learnt,
and the third would have had a presupposition about usefulness if the
words 'if any' had been removed. The main disadvantage claimed for
presupposition questions is that they may help the informant to open
up, particularly when the material being investigated is either
uncomfortable or embarrassing. (For example, if there are criticisms to
be voiced about an individual's boss, of if there is some personal failing
of the informant which is of relevance.) The main disadvantages of
these questions are that they can sometimes put words into the informant's mouth, and the very crudeness of the presuppositions themselves
may be resented by perceptive informants.

The recording of interviews follows some of the guidelines above
about recorded observations. Provided that it does not inhibit the

informant it is always useful to have a tape recorder running during the interview. But note taking provides an essential complement to tape recordings. This is not only because it can help to identify crucial passages on the recording, not simply because there may be others in the world who have equally disastrous attempts at making electronic recordings work as myself, but also because note taking can be a very significant part of the dynamics of an interview. When the interviewer is writing notes this may provide space for the informant to think: selective note taking can also be used to indicate what the interviewer considers to be important, and less important, pieces of information, and hence can be used as a means of control (if that is what is wanted); and the procedure of reading back notes that have been written to the informant can provide both further clarification and increased accuracy of the written record.

Finally, by way of summary, it is worth listing a few pros and cons for interviews used as a method in evaluation. On the positive side, interviews can be both deep and flexible, and the opportunity to clarify meanings in both directions implies that the communication involved should be quite accurate. Interviews (especially informal ones) seem to be a much more natural way of gathering data when people are on hand – such as attending a course or programme. The obvious sense of using them to gather data in 'real' time means that they may be particularly suited to evaluations that are intended to serve the purposes of *improving* or *learning*. This is not to say that they do not have relevance to *proving*, particularly when information is to be gathered from people, such as bosses, with whom little previous contact has been established by the evaluator; but such studies which concentrate upon outcomes have the obvious disadvantage of being rather time consuming and expensive when based on interviews. This is the first of two of the cons that I have in mind about the use of interviews. The second is little more than a feeling; that there are often some very elaborate rituals and games that are played within interviews (such as giving the interviewer what he or she wants), but which are neither understood nor discussed much in the literature.

I encountered a recent example of this from a research study into the role of hospital administrators in the UK where data obtained from interviews seemed to have very little relationship to detailed observational studies of what they did in their work (Cunliffe, 1985). One of the reasons for these discrepancies seemed to be that during interviews the administrators gave the 'official' line about their roles (espoused theories), but over longer periods of time they naturally slipped back to their natural practices (theory-in-use) (Argyris and Schon, 1974), Recent examples of the inability of opinion polls to predict electoral behaviour have also been explained by the tendency to give socially-accepted answers in face-to-face interviews. Thus, although people do not seem to be deliberately dishonest in most evaluation interviews, there is still quite a high chance of distortions happening for perceptual

or political reasons. This, of course, is a drawback shared with questionnaires as data collection methods, and is one area where in theory the
more objective tests and scales do have some advantage. (On the hon-
esty issue, one of the major advantages of 'shared' interviews is that
both perceptual and political problems can be explored jointly by both
evaluator and informant, thus leading, perhaps, to greater accuracy and
understanding on both sides.)

Repertory grid technique

Repertory grids have been used in a number of evaluation studies
during recent years. The general principles to be employed in completing a grid are fairly tightly prescribed since they are based on an
elaborate and explicit psychological theory (Kelly, 1955). The starting
assumption of Kelly's personal construct theory is that people behave
and act according to how they classify and interpret what is going on
around them. It follows from this that it should be particularly useful
to identify (and measure) how people perceive objects, events, relationships, etc., and the repertory grid is one of a number of techniques
devised to do this.

One of the reasons for the popularity of organizational applications of
the repertory grid is that it provides quantitative methods of perceptions
which are otherwise very ill-defined and intangible. It is also extremely
flexible once the basic methodology of completing a grid is understood.
It is possible to adapt the content so that it may be applied to almost
whatever situation the investigator wishes to consider. This adapt-
ability, and the promise of quantitative measurements, has resulted in
some enthusiasm about its potential for evaluation studies, particularly
where it is hoped to *prove* that particular changes have taken place as
a result of training and development. Although the grid has a lot to
offer in evaluation studies, it seems that studies based on these aims
are unrealistic in their expectations of what the grid can do. As will be
illustrated in the example below (see Figure 5.11) it is of rather more
value on a reflexive/reflective basis, where it may be used as a contribution to the *learning* process itself.

My own experience of using the repertory grid in an attempt to *prove*
the effects of training (Easterby-Smith and Ashton, 1975) showed that
this was to some extent possible, but the results produced were neither
in the direction nor area anticipated beforehand. In particular, it was
found that there were more differences between a group of trainees
and a control group supposedly matched on all available criteria (see
Chapter 2), than there were changes to either group over the period of a
developmental programme lasting many months. The main discernible
change over this period was that the 'control' group, who did not
participate in the developmental programme appeared to have become
closer to their bosses, while the experimental group, who attended the

	Significant events in the programme (ELEMENTS)				
Elements construed 'in terms of what it was about these incidents which gave you these feelings'	Leaving the initial interview	First meeting with other participants	End of second workshop	Second tutorial	'Present state' on my project
	①	②	③	④	⑤

(Pair)	(Singleton)	1	2	3	4	5
123 discouraged involvement 1 2 3 4 5	encouraged involvement	5	3	2	4	5
245 focused 1 2 3 4 5	Unfocused	2	4	5	2	2
135 enabling progress 1 2 3 4 5	blocking progress	1	3	4	2	2
345 encouraged analysis 1 2 3 4 5	encouraged feeling	3	4	5	2	2
134 arouses curiosity 1 2 3 4 5	doesn't arouse curiosity	2	2	4	2	2

CONSTRUCTS

Figure 5.11 Repertory grid based on experience in a postgraduate programme

developmental programme, appeared to have become more distant from their bosses. This result clearly showed the ability of the repertory grid to yield the unexpected, but its relevance seems to be more towards *improving* the quality of future development programmes by increasing the involvement of bosses while trainees were on the programme (this was subsequently done with some success). However, this study was quite elaborate and time consuming; its ability to demonstrate changes, perceptual or otherwise, for participants was not comprehensive; and therefore I think it would be unwise to consider such applicants of the repertory grid as the answer to the problem of proving the value of training. In my view its main strength lies in attempts to *improve* training and development, and especially in assisting the *learning* of individuals involved. The following illustrations are intended to demonstrate this.

Examples of repertory grids

There are three main features to a repertory grid:

1   A set of *elements* which are the things, people, or situations to be examined.
2   a set of *constructs* which are pairs of statements used by the respondent to compare and contrast the elements selected.
3   a *linking* mechanism, normally ticks or crosses or a series of rating scales which demonstrate how each of the elements are construed on each of the constructs obtained.

A simple example of the first two features might be to consider three makes of motor car: Ford, Volvo and Honda. These would constitute a set of three elements. One of the most common ways of obtaining constructs is to derive them from three such elements (known as 'triading') by deciding in what way two of the elements are similar to each other, and yet different from the third. This should produce a word or phrase describing the similarity between the pair, and a *contrasting* word or phrase describing what it is that makes the third one distinct from the initial pair. Thus one person might look at these three elements and decide that Ford and Volvo are most alike in that they are both *European car manufacturers*, whereas Honda is different in being a *Japanese manufacturer of cars*. Another person might consider the triad and decide that Ford and Honda were most alike in having *lower prices*, whereas Volvo has an *image of being expensive*.

The above example was relatively straightforward, as grids go. The following example (see Figure 5.11) has two added levels of complexity. It was completed by a participant halfway through a two-year postgraduate programme in management learning, and was based on significant experiences of that individual while involved in the programme.

The first additional complexity was that the elements were not specified precisely (as in the case of Ford, Volvo and Honda); the individual was simply asked to identify particular events which fell into the general category 'of being significant to her'. The second added level of complexity was that these elements were not simply construed in isolation, but in terms of what it was about them which gave rise to particularly strong feelings in this participant. It will be seen in the example that each of the constructs derived from these elements (the numbers of the elements comprising the triad are given to the left of each construct) has been turned into a five-point rating scale. Taking the first construct, the number 1 would indicate that a particular event had *discouraged involvement*. Number 5 would indicate that the particular event had *encouraged involvement*, and that numbers in between would indicate various graduations between these two poles. By rating each of the elements on each of the bi-polar scales, the grid is thus built up into a 5 × 5 matrix. People who are new to the repertory grid but would like to experiment with it themselves, would do well to consult one of several more comprehensive sources on this topic (Bannister and Fransella, 1971; Easterby-Smith, 1980b; Stewart and Stewart, 1981b).

The analysis and interpretation of a small grid such as the one in Figure 5.11 can be done largely by eye and there is no need for computers or other forms of mechanical assistance. Nevertheless, it is necessary to start with the numbers in the matrix, and it is most instructive to look for similarities and differences in the rows and columns of the matrix. Thus by inspecting the columns of the matrix it will be seen that the ratings given to elements 4 and 5 are almost identical, indicating that these two events were experienced in very similar ways. Element number 1 is quite similar to these two (there being only two single point differences in the ratings for element 1 and element 5), whereas element 3, and to a lesser extent element 2, exhibit very different patterns. Although elements 2 and 3 are relatively close to each other on the first four constructs, there is a larger difference on the fifth: the 'First meeting with other participants' apparently *aroused curiosity*, whereas the 'End of second workshop' did not. Further fine distinctions can be made between the experiences of these various events by comparing the numbers in the column, although naturally how far one goes should depend upon how finely the respondent is able to differentiate between adjacent points on the rating scale.

Turning now to the relationships between the constructs as indicated by the rows of figures, two main groupings are apparent. There is a reasonably strong similarity between the first, third and fifth construct (assuming that the polarity of the first construct is reversed, thus making ones, fives; twos, fours; and so on). Thus, events on the programme (elements) which are felt to *encourage involvement* are also experienced as *enabling progress* and *arousing curiosity*. The second grouping comprises the second and fourth construct, and this is an interesting one because it does not include the straightforward evaluative element of the other three constructs. In this case, events that are experienced as *focused* are the ones that also encourage analysis, whereas those that are *unfocused* are the ones likely to *encourage feeling*. Again the analysis of these constructs can be taken further, but this discussion is intended merely to provide a flavour for what can be done.

So what is the value of going through this process? For the individual concerned in the above example, it seemed to have several kinds of value. Firstly, it was a useful way to help her review her progress through the programme up to that point. Secondly, the discipline of having to complete the grid in the prescribed way forced her to think in areas and ways which she had not previously employed: that in itself was of value if the purpose of the grid was to help her learn. Finally, the analysis and interpretation of this small grid helped her to bring together some ideas (*focus*, to use her own term), about how she experiences and judges a learning event.

Thus, there are a number of ways in which this grid was able to contribute to the individual's learning, and such exercises, when designed appropriately, are invariably of value at this level. The grid would also be of use to a course tutor wishing to *improve* the programme on future occasions. For example, a number of ideas might be gleaned from this grid about why initial meetings on the programme did not work particularly well: the need to encourage more genuine involvement and to provide greater focusing at that stage might be two points to take up. Moreover, the tutor might gain even more understanding about what had gone wrong and what could be rectified through talking with the respondent about why she had rated the event in that particular way.

When the Figure 5.11 grid design was used every participant produced a totally different grid. It is the ability of the grid to probe deeply into unique experiences and perceptions which is its greatest strength. This is why it has great value in assisting the learning process, and to a lesser extent is helping to *improve* the structures and processes of learning. Nevertheless, the uniqueness and unpredictability of the data produced makes it extremely hard for it to be used to make generalized statements about a particular programme or activity, and thus to use this evaluation instrument in an *improving* manner, for the programme as a whole.

Critical incident techniques

The main principle underlying the critical incident technique is that in everyday life or work people fall into habits and patterns of behaviour which become to them perfectly normal and unremarkable. To the complete outsider these patterns, such as a deference to authority, or acceptance of rules and procedures which are obviously dysfunctional, may seem a little curious. But insiders are not likely to become aware that many of their actions are quite arbitrary and ritualized unless something exceptional takes place to punctuate these patterns of normality. For example, if somebody suddenly refuses to obey an instruction from a superior manager this may open many questions about the basis for accepting that manager's authority. Another celebrated example was when Lord Weinstock decreed in GEC that all meetings (other than statutory board meetings) were to be banned for six months. Thereafter it was possible to decide which kinds of meetings would really be in the company's interests, and which meetings could be dispensed with.

Thus the principle of critical incident technique is to focus upon the unusual, the discontinuities, and the exceptional circumstances. In this way it is intended to throw light upon the realities of normal behaviour and circumstances (Ruddock, 1981).

Although the first published account of the technique being used was in 1953, perhaps the most widely known application of this technique was in the research leading to Frederick Herzberg's two factor theory of motivation. Herzberg's research was based on asking about 200 employees to think of specific times when they felt particularly good or particularly bad about their jobs, and then to describe in as much detail as possible the conditions that apparently led to them having these feelings. Through an analysis of these 'critical' incidents and the associated explanations, Herzberg and his associates were able to derive a new way of understanding why people do, or do not, perform well at work. (Herzberg, Mausner and Snyderman, 1959.)

The five elements in the example of a repertory grid provided earlier are also critical incidents in the experience of that participant during the postgraduate programme. These critical incidents focus on what has been described above as the *process* of the programme (see Chapter 3), and in a way the repertory grid provided a rather more tightly prescribed way of understanding the effect of these incidents. Likewise the critical incident technique could be used to focus upon inputs, context, or administration of a particular programme, but it has rather greater advantage when focusing on the outcomes. This is because the logic of much evaluation aimed at *proving* assumes that something must have changed as the result of training or development. This happens to coincide with the concentration of critical incidents on changes from normality. Thus bosses or ex-participants on courses can be asked to focus on one or two specific examples where a crisis has been handled differently, or where a procedural change has been made, presumably as a result of something that took place on a course. It is then possible to probe into why this change came about, what its effect was, and so on. Moreover, if one has the time it is also possible to triangulate by asking a number of different people about the same incident (boss, colleagues, subordinates) in order to build up a more complete picture.

An obvious strength of the critical incident technique is its ability to identify issues and events, and then to dig into their circumstances in some depth. An additional advantage of the technique is that it produces anecdotes and examples which are very close to normal managerial language. The data yielded from critical incidents may have high credibility when one is trying to convince senior managers or stakeholders about the worthwhileness of a particular course or programme. Thus the critical incident technique can provide a very useful complement to a more comprehensive evaluation study, regardless of what other data collection techniques are being employed.

The main limitation of the technique is that it, inevitably, uses only a very small sample of the total range of incidents that may have taken place, and of course this sampling is dependent upon whatever the respondent decides is of significance. The high degree of control thus allowed to the respondent over the content of the critical incident may therefore be unacceptable to researchers and evaluators who feel that they alone should be the guardians and arbitrators of objective truth. For others, it is not such a bad thing at all to make use more fully of the skill and judgement of respondents. Not only are they largely responsible for the content of these critical incidents, but the procedure for providing this information is rather less tightly prescribed than in the case of the repertory grid. That is why critical incidents have been located somewhat to the right of the repertory grid technique in Figure 5.1.

Self-reports

In this case a further degree of freedom is allowed to the informant who is encouraged to provide whatever data and comments he or she wishes within a general area of interest or in response to a trigger question. In some cases the medium of response is suggested; in others this is of little relevance.

Self-reports have achieved some respectability as research evidence when collected in the form of diaries (Carlson, 1951; Stewart, 1967). But Mintzberg (1973) criticizes them as sources of evidence to understand managerial work on the grounds that they are rather inflexible, that they do require the diarist to be a highly-skilled observer of his or her work, and they have difficulty coping with rapidly changing and short-run incidents.

These are problems when one wishes to use diaries as a source of 'objective' data; but if the intention is to use such diaries to assist the *learning* process, then the problem is greatly reduced. In the UK, the National Examination Board in Supervisory Studies (NEBSS) and the Business Education Council (BEC) both encouraged the use of learning diaries on part-time post-experience courses. In many cases these diaries formed part of the final assessment of such courses, being judged on the ability of the diarist to reflect upon his or her own learning processes, and to establish links both ways between the content of the course and the experiences of working in a job. It is generally assumed by proponents of this method that the assessment of diaries acts as a spur to their completion, and that therefore it provides a net contribution to the overall learning process.

Learning diaries may be used to demonstrate the effect of particular courses, or to help in the improvement of future courses, but they are more normally seen to be of benefit primarily to the diarist. But there are other methods, often using tape recordings or letters, which provide a more open format for providing reports on the effect and experience of educational processes and procedures. The research study by Burgoyne (1975) used one simple trigger question to explore the way in which informants formed judgements about the value of a postgraduate course, and this judgemental process was recorded on tape. The trigger question was: 'What is the value to you of your attendance at the course and has it been worthwhile from your point of view?' Analysis of the data yielded by this question indicated a range of concepts of value, including: financial, occupational, intrinsic enjoyment of the course, and enhancement of self-respect. The study did not enable an overall judgement to be reached about the value of the course; indeed it demonstrated that criteria of value vary quite significantly from one individual to another, and therefore that any single dimensional judgement about value is likely to be a gross simplification.

Burgoyne was present when his informants taped their comments about the value of the course; but it quite possible to send a tape through the post and ask for some comments to be made before the tape is returned to the evaluator. Jameson (1980) used this approach to follow up participants after a small business course and made a comparison between the data yielded by such tapes and that produced by interviews, mailed questionnaires and letters. The latter I would classify as another self-report method since they are normally sent in response to a rather generally worded enquiry from the evaluator or they are altogether unsolicited. Although her sample was relatively small (thirty-two participants), Jameson's results did demonstrate quite strong differences between the four methods: tapes and letters produced quite a substantial amount of information of reasonable quality; they were both better than questionnaires, but not as good as interviews for generating data. On the other hand they were far less expensive both in terms of time and travel expenses than interviews when following up after a course.

Self-reports have much in common with critical incident technique, although they do not provide such focused information and allow even greater freedom for the informant to decide what is important and how to express it. The freedom of self-reports means that they may be used to serve a number of purposes, and to focus on any aspect of the training and developmental process without any one context being markedly preferable to the others. Nevertheless one of the attractive features about self-reports is that they are minimally influenced by the interests of the evaluator/tutor or by the institutions involved with a particular programme. That is why Jameson chose these methods when attempting to do a 'goal free' evaluation study. Whether the potential independence of self-reports provides adequate compensation for their lack of precise focus must be for the user to judge.

Consumer evaluation

Whereas a high degree of freedom is allowed to the informant in the case of self-reports, consumer evaluation implies that freedom is *taken* by participants and clients to make their own judgements. There is another difference between the two: self-reports are generally provided by individuals, but collated and used by the evaluators or tutors; consumer evaluation implies full control being taken by participants both for providing information and for making sense of it.

Consumer evaluation requires that students or clients perceive themselves as a group with some organizational capability. In this sense three main kinds of grouping might be distinguished: companies or organizations as clients; student bodies as a whole; and groups of participants directly involved with a particular programme. In companies or organizations where management training and development is a regular and perhaps costly feature, reports after attendance on courses are often institutionalized. However, it appears that considerable use is not made of these procedures, possibly because their purpose is not clear and they therefore evolve into rituals (Easterby-Smith, Braiden and Ashton, 1980).

For a number of years the British Institute of Management (BIM) provided a course assessment service (Wilson, 1970). The service gave ratings on a number of publicly offered courses based on returns from BIM members. The main relevance of this service, and by implication much of the internal company evaluation procedures, was to help people decide whether or not to make use of particular courses and programmes. But the most effective forms of evaluation by companies acting as clients tend to take place informally in response to some perceived crisis or change in policy. These are based upon the time-honoured practice of 'informed prejudice' and on the informal information channels that most senior managers find necessary to establish.

The second form of consumer evaluation consists of student evaluation of their teachers and professors at university or in other educational establishments. This is carried out in a highly rigorous and quantified manner in the USA, where all faculty can be graded according to their student ratings; less sophisticated approaches are adopted in the UK. At Lancaster University an annual 'Alternative Prospectus' is prepared by the Students' Union which provides feedback on undergraduate courses run throughout the university. Although this, as with many other student evaluations, can easily be dismissed by staff and the administration on methodological grounds, its effect cannot be overlooked when it is distributed to first-year students in the period they are to choose their registrations for second- and third-year courses.

Whereas the first two forms of consumer evaluation are directed towards helping future students and clients to decide whether they should become involved or continue to be involved with a particular programme (mainly about *proving*), the third form of consumer evaluation may have some relevance to improving future programmes, to letting off steam if that is appropriate, or simply providing a light-hearted finish to a particular course. These are the review groups which are often established at the end of a substantial residential programme with the aims of reviewing what has been learnt, what has worked well, and what has not worked so well. Although at one level this type of review may be seen as frivolous, it is important that people are able to look back upon developmental experiences as positive ones, whenever this is possible.

These three forms of consumer evaluation have been described in the order of their ability to generate changes, and this is largely a matter of the balance of power between providers and consumers in each case. Of the three, the data produced by various forms of student evaluation are probably the most accurate. It is unfortunate, but rather inevitable, that many educational establishments try to reduce the credibility and impact of such evaluations.

Conclusion

This chapter has considered the range of data collection methods, or classes of methods, which may be used in different circumstances and for different evaluation purposes.

Those wishing to apply any of them in practice may also be advised to consult some of the more specialized sources that have been indicated in the text. However, before finishing the chapter there are two general issues that need to be considered briefly: the first being of relevance primarily to this and the previous chapter; and the second of relevance to this and the following chapter – thus providing some kind of bridge.

Combining methods and media

This first issue is about whether it is right and proper to combine methods and media which make quite different assumptions about the nature of the phenomena they are considering, or about who is controlling the data collection process. For example, Parlett and Hamilton (1972) in their classic paper make a distinction between traditional evaluation approaches based on the 'agricultural-botany paradigm' and illuminative evaluation based on the 'social-anthropological paradigm'. The point about paradigms, as described by Kuhn (1962) is that they cannot and should not be mixed: data obtained within one scientific paradigm will either contradict, or will have no bearing whatever upon data gained from another scientific paradigm. It therefore does not add to the overall store of knowledge if data is combined from more than one paradigm. Fielding and Fielding (1986) advocate the use of both quantitative and qualitative methods when conducting social research and illustrate how this was done when researching the British National Front. In relation to evaluation, Reichardt and Cook (1979) also examined the problem, and concluded that there are many overlaps in the kinds of data yielded and conclusions that are possible. Although there were still some differences, these were largely ones of degree. Their advice is to adopt whatever evaluation methods, and combinations of methods, are likely to be most productive in view of the aims of the evaluation study. A combination of qualitative and quantitative methods has particular advantages if the evaluation study is intended to serve multiple purposes, but even when being used for the same purpose, a combination of methods may provide complementary perspectives. In addition, if one assumes that all methods have their own particular bias then a combination of different methods may be used to reduce the bias inherent in any one method (Hamblin 1974; Patton, 1980). When all is said and done, evaluation is a rather 'murky' business and the evaluator should be prepared to use whatever methods prove to be helpful. It is important to be aware of the different issues underlying these, and of the possible problems which may thereby be created, but the evaluator can ill-afford to be too precious over his or her methodology. The final caveat about combinations of methodologies is a practical one too: this is that methodological triangulation, as Patton puts it, may be prohibitively expensive both in terms of time and money. On that basis it might be worth giving a little more thought to selecting the most appropriate method, rather than a range of methods in the hope that one or two of them will provide what is wanted.

Ethics

The second issue is one of *ethics*. It is possible to raise this issue but by no means to dismiss it. Three ethical questions are pertinent to the above discussions about data collection methods:

1   What is the basis of the contract, psychological or otherwise, whereby one person is able to gather information from another?
2   In what senses can such data be treated as confidential?
3   Who does, or should, own the results?

With regard to contracts, these are very rarely stated explicitly, at least when the evaluator and informant are confronting each other, and it seems that each falls quite naturally into the roles that they have learnt for researchers and the one who is researched into – one receives and the other gives. As someone who is normally in the researcher/evaluator role, I have become acutely aware on occasions when I have been on the receiving end of this process just how much was taken for granted. The problem is that the more explicit the contract, the more troublesome may be the restrictions placed on access and areas of investigation (Becker, 1979; Reickhardt and Cook, 1979; Punch, 1986). Furthermore, if one adopts a conflict view of society where it is natural for people to be suspicious of others and to hide their own reasons and intents wherever possible, it can be argued that the only way to gather data of any validity at all is for the researcher to operate in a covert manner (Douglas, 1976).

Whether or not explicit contracts are formed between evaluators and informants, there is likely to be some understanding on the part of both about the extent to which information should be treated in confidence. This forms the second ethical question, about confidentiality, and it may be seen at two levels: confidentiality between informants, and confidentiality for clients. With regard to informants, my assumption, which is made explicit whenever possible, is that no information provided by an individual should be conveyed to another individual or group in a way that could identify the source of that information, unless explicit permission has been given for this to take place. The extent to which one can use information from one person to prompt or trigger information from another person, or the extent to which one can triangulate accounts between different individuals, depends upon how easily individuals can be identified by others on the basis of their opinions – and therefore to avoid violating this principle of confidentiality, one may need to know a lot about the norms and relationships between different informants. As with the problem of access, considerable sensitivity is required on the part of the evaluator if this is to be handled appropriately. As far as clients are concerned (i.e. the people who have legitimized, authorized, paid for, or asked for evaluation to be done) my assumption likewise is that no information should be made available to any further parties in a form that could in any way identify the client, unless explicit permission has been given for this. But this returns us to the problem discussed earlier, about determining precisely who the client is. Should one regard as clients only those who sponsor the evaluation financially or should one widen the definition to include different groups of stakeholders too?

The third question, about ownership, raises similar problems. If, for example, an interview is carried out and it is recorded upon tape, who owns the data on the tape? Is it the interviewer, the informant, or the person who is paying for the evaluation to be done? As with the other issues, there is no easy answer to this question, but those who get involved in evaluations should give some thought to it. Apart from the fact that it has bearings on confidentiality, it has implications for how such data might be used in the future.

6 Interpreting and using evaluations

The previous chapter reviewed a number of ways of gathering evaluative information about management training and education. The next question follows fairly naturally: having gathered all this data, what is going to happen to it and how might it be used?

According to many of the earlier writers on evaluation of management training, there is not much of a problem here. Hamblin (1974) and Warr, Bird and Rackham (1970), seem to regard this merely as a technical matter of providing feedback at the end of the evaluation study. On the other hand Patton (1978) sees the potential usability of evaluation data being determined largely by what has, or has not, taken place at the *beginning* of the study. In his view it is crucial to start by identifying and organizing the key decision makers and information users, to find out what questions they have which they would like answered, and to involve these people in key decisions whenever possible. This advice is offered with large scale 'funded' projects in mind, where the main emphasis is upon *proving* something about the programme, or possibly on *improving* certain aspects of it.

Although Patton's ideas and advice are of considerable use in thinking about the 'utilization' (his term) of evaluations in the areas of management education, training and development, there are three features which differentiate these forms of evaluation from those with which Patton is most familiar: first, they tend to be on a much smaller scale; second, they may often be aimed at the purpose of *learning*, in addition to the purposes Patton normally considers; and third, they are more likely to take place within or close to a specific organizational context. The latter point forms a fairly strong contrast with Patton's work, which tends to be within the more diffuse context of federal legislation or local authority programmes where 'political' aspects can be related rather closely to the activities of various elected or appointed individuals. In these cases accountability and public scrutiny are regular occurrences. By contrast most organizations, whether private or public, tend to shun external scrutiny whenever possible. They, and management training programmes (which often become organizational entities in themselves), can become very effective at managing their boundaries – through the control of information dissemination, personnel selection and induction, and occasionally through appealing to unique histories and traditions. The more successful organizations are in this respect, the more they are likely to develop idiosyncratic ways of doing things and of operating internally. These idiosyncratic ways of operating are often referred to as organizational cultures (Handy, 1976), and it is the purpose of this chapter to demonstrate how important is a knowledge of specific organizational cultures when one wishes to ensure that some use is made of evaluations (assuming that the people who are in a position to make use of these evaluations are other than the evaluators themselves).

In particular it is the typical judgement and/or decision-making processes in any particular organization which are likely to have the greatest effect on whether evaluation results get used. Consequently this chapter will start by looking at judgemental and decision-making processes in organizations and other bounded communities in general. It will then extend the discussion to political aspects of evaluation utilization before concluding with a brief discussion of some of the issues that these political features raise for the role of people engaged in evaluative activities.

Decision-making processes: some alternative assumptions

Management education and development programmes are normally related quite closely to organizations – whether they be sponsors, providers, or clients – and it is therefore likely that organizational decision-making styles will affect the use to be made of evaluative activities. How one decides to tackle the problem of 'utilization' therefore depends somewhat on the assumptions one holds about the way organizations operate, and about how decisions are taken within them. This section starts with a review of assumptions about organizational decision-making processes in general, before discussing some of the specific implications of these for those wishing to ensure that some use is made of evaluation. I should also make it clear that this is in no way intended as a comprehensive review of theories of organizational behaviour; it is merely intended to provide some selective pointers for the discussion which follows later in the chapter.

There are two areas of competing assumptions that seem to be of relevance here. The first is between what might be called *determinism*, and *agency*. By this I mean the question of whether what takes place in an organization is largely determined in advance by social or organizational structures, where the actions of individuals are seen as largely constrained by the roles, hierarchy, and relationships at work; or whether more complete explanations and understanding of what takes place can be reached through concentrating on the aspirations, intentions, and actions of individual members of the organization.

The deterministic perspective seems to be rather more inflexible and is held by either those who wish to justify and maintain the *status quo* (by claiming that it is not really possible to influence it much anyway), or by those who are strongly opposed to the *status quo*, and who argue that the only viable way of changing it is to dismantle all existing social and organizational structures, and to start anew. I find the 'agency' view more optimistic in that it maintains the possibility of individuals making significant changes and improvements to organizational and social affairs if they set their minds to it – and it also seems that it is necessary for those people carrying out evaluations to accept something of this view if they wish to see the role of evaluation being any more than an opportunity for people to 'let off steam'.

The second kind of debate, particularly if one takes a predominantly 'agency' view of organization, is about the way the goals, and decisions about the goals, of the organization come into being. At one end of the debate are those who regard goal formation as relatively uncontentious: they assume that it is possible to conduct a rational evaluation of options and alternatives which results in a *consensus* over what should be done between all the parties involved. In contrast are those who see continual *conflicts* taking place between individuals and interest groups within organizations about decisions over goals and resource allocation.

If one adopts a consensus view of organizational decision making then one would expect that the likelihood of evaluation results being *used* would depend mainly on the technical quality of the design and implementation of study. Those who adopt more of a conflict perspective will see evaluation inevitably as part of the ongoing political processes of the organization or community in question. Indeed, it seems highly likely that evaluation studies will get dragged into the political arena since evaluations are primarily about generating or recycling information; and information, as Perrow (1971) and Pettigrew (1973) tell us, is one of the most crucial elements in organizational politics. As Patton comments on this problem for academic evaluators:

> The traditionally academic values of many social scientists leave them to want to be non-political in their research. Yet they always want to effect government decisions. The evidence is that they cannot have it both ways. To be innocent of the political nature of evaluation research is to become a pawn in someone else's game, wittingly or unwittingly – or perhaps more commonly, to miss the game altogether.
>
> (Patton, 1978 p. 46.)

This is not to say that the technical aspects of evaluation are unimportant. Indeed, being able to demonstrate that a reasonably technical job has been done is one of the major political cards that one might play in trying to ensure that someone takes notice of the results. But I find that it is these political aspects in relation to evaluation which are particularly interesting, and which have received only limited attention in the literature in the past, and I therefore think it is appropriate to devote the bulk of the chapter to such aspects. The discussion of the political aspects of evaluation will then be followed by some suggestions about how the interpretation and utilization of evaluations can be helped from a technical point of view. The chapter concludes with a brief discussion of some of the issues that evaluation poses for the role of the evaluator.

A model of organizational politics

The model proposed here for looking at organizations combines elements of the consensus and conflict perspectives discussed above. Most organizations have unique value systems, which are shared by, or at least dominate among, large numbers of employees working for them. One well known organization with a strongly shared value system is IBM, where the notion of 'excellence in all we do' provides a unifying ideology among employees. This, along with related value systems such as 'close to the customer' and 'sticking with the knitting', features strongly in the Peters and Waterman (1982) study of highly-successful organizations. Although subsequent history has shown that the particular culture of IBM may not always provide a recipe for success, it is still clear that many modern companies encourage strong task-oriented value systems. In other organizations the dominant value systems may be more traditionalist or role-orientated, and reflect on the credibility of managers who have, or have not, served apprenticeships appropriate to that organization as gas fitters, research chemists or sales representatives, etc. The point about the latter kind of value system is that it remains dominant over other alternative value systems, primarily because those individuals who identify themselves with these viewpoints or pedigrees occupy and are able to maintain the more senior positions in the organization (Easterby-Smith, 1979).

In some organizations (often those that do not see themselves under much threat or in much competition), the alternative value systems are not greatly in evidence. In other cases, particularly during periods of crisis, there may be very strong conflict between different views of what the organization should be doing and what it should become. At the time of writing, universities in the UK are agonizing over whether to devote resources towards developing excellence in research while being very selective in recruiting students, or whether to opt for the mass student market. Both options are risky, but there is a logic pressing the older universities along the former route, and most of the newer universities (former polytechnics) along the latter. Such conflicts do not take place in a vacuum. Looking at this through the *agency* perspective one would see groups of individuals, or departments, aligning themselves behind one value system or another, and this would be reflected both in the way they attempt to influence decisions, and in the way they interpret information that is of relevance to those decisions. Thus, in the case of a large public sector organization facing privatization, people in marketing functions might take every opportunity to introduce data about external competition as evidence of the need for greater resources and priorities to be placed in their area; and people in technical functions may try to concentrate management's attention on the absolute need to introduce the most modern hardware into the company as soon as it is available.

Competing interpretations of what is right and appropriate for an organization may not only come from different formal departments or divisions, they may also cut across the organization on social or personal lines. For example, a frequent conflict in industrial companies in the early 1970s was between those who felt the company had a responsibility to maintain employment for all its employees, and those who felt the company had a responsibility to its shareholders to cut its employment costs as quickly and extensively as possible. This debate parallels the recent political debate in Europe about whether it is in each country's interest to submit to central fiscal control, and to some extent political control, or whether to go it alone. Positions taken by different groups depend much on ideological and historical factors. Such values and beliefs may be fairly deep seated and enduring, therefore leading to fairly stable groupings of people within the organization – such as those who are generally positive about training and development, and those who see it as having little relevance to the ultimate success of the company. Then there always seems to be considerable individual manoeuvring which may not be based on any thought-out value positions, rather upon personal interests. Depending on the organization and its circumstances, individuals may be tempted to obtain greater rewards for themselves, or added control over resources (for example, through promotions or 'empire' building). Individual manoeuvring may be more or less evident within any particular organization, but to the extent that it is present it will have a bearing upon how evaluation studies are interpreted and used.

Implications where there are shared value systems

Every organization seems to have its own style of handling information and communications internally. For example, in some companies everything has to be circulated in the form of written memoranda, or in some it is more efficient to telephone people than to send notes to them, and in others the more important communications take place in coffee rooms, bars, or restaurants. It therefore seems important that if evaluation reports are to be taken seriously they need to take account of the way stakeholders are accustomed to receive information, and therefore to form judgements. Three general procedures are quite common, although in any single organization one of them will tend to be predominant.

Firstly, there are organizations that rely very heavily on *scientific* forms of information. Written reports abound, and quantitative indices of performance exist for most features of the company's, and individual's, activities. Whether or not such quantified indices are really measuring what they are supposed to measure, or whether their existence contributes in any way to the overall performance of the organization, is immaterial to the present argument. The point is that evaluation reports presented to people within such cultures may be seen as suspect if they are not backed up by adequate statistics.

The second form of information may be labelled *bureaucratic*. In this case there is less reliance on substantiating claims with hard evidence, than on ensuring that information has come from the right, and legitimate, source. For the evaluator, this can mean ensuring that reports have the stamp of approval of very senior managers – which will therefore confirm a general legitimacy of the contents of a report – or it can mean making it clear that they themselves have the authority and legitimacy to gather information and make valid judgements (which is why outside evaluators from academic management schools may be preferred in this case).

The third form of information consists of *anecdotes*. Such anecdotes are not normally written down (as in the two cases above), but form part of the natural conversational exchanges between the members of the organization. And anecdotes, for example stories about horrific (or enlightening) experiences on courses, are often selected by the informant in order to demonstrate a particular point of view. In some respects anecdotal forms of information may be very similar to the critical incident technique discussed in the previous chapter. The problem comes, however, when anecdotes are used not to convey a fair and balanced picture of what took place but as part of a competitive game along the lines of 'ain't it awful'. The implications here for evaluators are that if they wish to produce reports in any written form at all, these are more likely to be acceptable if they contain direct quotations, stories, and incidents, preferably provided by people known to the stakeholders (if this does not create problems for the confidentiality of informants).

One further point to support the significance of the normal information system within an organization comes from Patton's (1978) research into the relationship between the 'validity' of evaluation studies, and the degree to which they were used by clients and 'decision makers'. This is that the various forms of validity as understood by researchers (i.e. whether the study has been conducted according to the best principles of scientific practice) are far less important than the *face* validity of results (i.e. whether the information has come from reliable sources, and whether the results fit with 'common sense' expectations).

The discussion above about the preferences for different types of information in different organizations bears on the question of whether or not any notice will be taken of evaluative information. The next question to be considered is whether there is likely to be a consistent bias in different organizations when interpreting any evaluative information that is already seen to be both acceptable and credible. A paper by Gibson (1983) points out how different stages of group development within an educational programme may affect both judgements by participants of the programme itself, and the way they interpret any evaluative information that may be fed back to them (in a formative way) during the programme itself. Thus, for example, in a twelve-week executive programme, there may be clear expectations that structure and leadership should be provided by tutors during the 'forming' stage during the first week or so; but the same structuring role from tutors a few weeks further into the programme may be rejected when the group has developed its own norms of operation. Likewise the interpretation of any evaluative data generated by participants is likely to be very critical during what are regarded as normal phases of frustration and conflict in the programme. If such formative data are genuinely intended to lead to changes within the programme itself, there is some danger that judgements of 'crisis' identified during the more stormy (but natural) phases in development of the group may result in over reactions on the part of the programme management. This will in the long run be detrimental both to individual learning and to group development.

Gibson's (1983) paper considers the effect of interpretative and judgemental bias as it may vary within one group within the life of a single programme. Of course, such interpretative bias may be more consistent within organizations as a whole and between individuals. For example, if a one-week programme for managers on 'man management skills' receives an end-of-course rating of 3.8 on the scale illustrated below:

Poor	Adequate	Good	Very Good	Excellent
1	2	3	4	5

is this to be considered a good or bad result? Does it indicate that the programme should be changed, scrapped, or allowed to continue as it is? . . . A discussion between an optimist and a pessimist on the interpretation of this result might then go along the following lines:

Optimist – 'This result is really very good in comparison with similar human relations courses which specifically aim to develop participants' critical faculties.'
Pessimist – 'I don't agree. The average rating for all other short courses in our

institution is 4.5 on the same scale. No other course obtained such low ratings with such consistency. These results are quite unacceptable.'
Optimist – 'But you must accept that a lot of the people on our courses are sent precisely because they have some problems at work. On this occasion there were four members of the programme who resented being sent on it, and they were quite determined to be disruptive from the outset.'
Pessimist – 'If your subject is really human relations such real life problems should have made this particular course that much more interesting and successful.'
Optimist – 'But it was a very successful course . . .'

Clearly the main way of interpreting such quantitative data is in comparison with similar programmes, but in the absence of any pre-agreed criteria for interpretation it is likely that different judges will select different cases for comparison according to whatever conclusions they want to draw. Furthermore, one would expect the arguments of the optimist to prevail if they took place in an organization where senior managers were generally positively disposed to training and development, and the arguments of the pessimist to prevail in an organization that was placing great emphasis on efficiency and cost-cutting.

Implications where there are competing interpretations and values

At this point it is necessary to review the different expectations and hopes that various stakeholders may have from a particular evaluation. For example, a training manager may be interested in the results of evaluation studies if they can help in control of unruly training staff; a central administrator may be more interested in evaluations which could result in the establishment of more standardized procedures, methods, and programmes; a management development manager may be hoping that evaluation will demonstrate the absolute necessity of greater resources being provided for his function; or a trainee on a programme may be hoping that it will encourage senior managers to let him or her put into practice some of the new ideas he or she has encountered and developed during a particular course. As Kotter and Lawrence (1974) point out, these expectations or 'agendas' may vary in their time horizon from short to long term: short-term agendas being relatively reactive and opportunistic, long-term agendas tending to be pro-active and far reaching. Of the four examples given above, the first two could be relatively long-term agendas, and the second two are likely to represent fairly short-term agendas.

People who hold relatively long-term agendas upon which the results of evaluation activities may have some bearing are likely to have strong views in advance about the desirable outcomes from the evaluation; and more so than those who have short-term agendas. (One other very common long-term agenda comes from trainers as stakeholders: 'To keep me in a job!') One way to find out what results people would really like to see from such a study is simply to ask them. They can always evade the question or dissemble if they wish. Another way is to ask other observers what it is that they think the main stakeholders are trying to achieve – and this is an area where the role of key informants (as mentioned earlier) can be exceedingly valuable.

Attempting to identify and interrelate the agendas of crucial stakeholders takes the evaluation somewhat beyond the position advocated by Patton (1978), where the crucial questions to find out from stakeholders are:

1 What it is that they want to know about the programme or activity in question?; and
2 How much difference it would make for them if they were able to obtain that information through an evaluation?

Admittedly a knowledge of the questions that people would like to have answered can give some good clues to the kind of answers that they would like to receive; but when dealing with the complex politics of organizations or learning communities, the evaluator should make more than casual observations of key stakeholders' motives and agendas.

In this respect there is a particular problem for people conducting evaluations within organizations or learning communities of which they are also members, since it will be hard for them to disengage from their own agendas (if they have any), and they will also be rather dependent upon their own selective information channels. And within the closed community of a management course such information channels may become exceptionally selective. For example, on one occasion in an important management programme two members of the faculty managed to present wholly contradictory reports of participants' reactions to a particular incident, and each had based his conclusions on conversations with quite a number of participants. It would seem, therefore, that on such a programme faculty members will develop contacts and information channels with people who are most likely to share and support their own views, both in general terms and with regard to specific incidents.

Senior managers who by the very nature of their jobs tend to be rather isolated from day-to-day activities, also seem to place particular premium upon informal information channels (and networks) (Kotter and Lawrence, 1974). This may also be reflected in a preference for anecdotal, rather than scientific or bureaucratic forms of information at senior levels of the organization. For example, I was discussing a middle management course with a director of a company, and how he had developed his attitudes towards it. It became quite clear in this discussion that he placed far more reliance upon the report of a close colleague who had attended this particular course in the role of a 'live case study' than he did on any information produced by the management training department itself. The immediate implication of this is that evaluators must recognize that there are natural information channels which, particularly at a senior level, tend to be far more influential than formal channels. Thus, even if evaluation reports are to be written in a formal sense it will greatly help their credibility if the most vital points contained within them can also have reached the ears of influential stakeholders through more informal channels.

There remain then two dilemmas for evaluators who are keen to ensure that some use is made of their efforts, and want to ensure that this is not too greatly distorted by political considerations. Firstly, if it becomes evident that crucial stakeholders have information channels that tend to provide highly distorted information, should the evaluator challenge this or simply make use of these channels for his or her own purposes? Perhaps the best way of dealing with this problem is to ensure that information does come through more 'balanced' channels in addition to the selective ones preferred by the stakeholders in question.

This leads to the second dilemma. What should the evaluator do if there are clear differences between interpretations provided by different information channels, or more generally between the results of an evaluation study and the outcomes that a particular stakeholder was hoping to hear? A cynical view of this is that for the sake of the evaluator's livelihood and credibility some amount of dissonance (but not too much) is both good and necessary, and one limiting factor upon the amount of dissonance that is acceptable to a stakeholder, without attempting to discredit the whole study, is the credibility that the evaluator brings to the role (see Figure 6.1).

Sometimes I have been surprised by how much people are willing to listen to, and pay for, bad news! The conclusion for the evaluator is that if the results of the study generally align with what most stakeholders are hoping to hear, there is no great problem, and they will be pleased to receive confirmation of what they always knew to be the case. If there is a divergence between results and what people had hoped for then there is little point beating about the bush, and in most cases such results will be accepted, perhaps grudgingly. What is important here is for the evaluator to be aware when the presentation of results is likely to create considerable dissonance. Being forewarned he or she may be more able to ensure that people are left with sufficient possibilities of saving face and this should significantly reduce the difficulties of the feedback session.

Gaining commitment to action

This section assumes that some type of action or changes are desirable as a result of a particular evaluation activity, although it should be noted that in many cases evaluation results will have been used quite adequately and correctly if *no* action is taken. One way of increasing

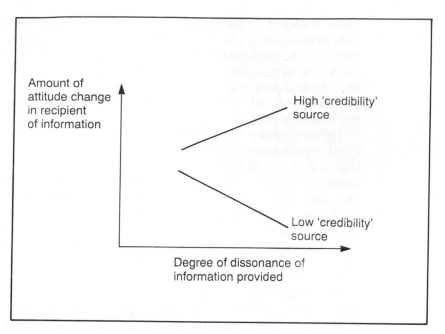

Figure 6.1   The influence of 'credibility' on the acceptance of dissonant information

people's commitment to take some action (and, incidentally, of reducing the possible problems of dissonance discussed in the previous section), is to make sure that final reports do not come as a great surprise to stakeholders. As Patton comments:

> Utilization does not centre around the final report. The final report is part of a total utilization process but in many cases it is a minor part. Evaluators who prefer to work diligently in the solitude of their offices until they can spring a final report on a waiting world may find that the world has passed them by. The reason is that evaluation feedback is most useful as part of a process of thinking about a programme, rather than as a one-shot information input.

(Patton, 1978, p. 264.)

Not only should stakeholders be kept informed of developments as far as is possible, but it is also worth involving them in taking input decisions too. As discussed earlier this might involve them in deciding what are the most important questions to be answered, agreeing what methods of data collection and analysis should be used, agreeing in advance what criteria will be employed for interpretation, and so on. If reports are to be produced, provided there is sufficient time for this, it is often worth producing several reports for different audiences or stakeholders. I should make it clear, however, that in no way should such reports attempt to provide different interpretations or selections of evidence. The main differences should be along the lines of emphasizing answers to questions of interest to one group of stakeholders or another, and in the language used and the amount of detail provided in such reports. This therefore takes account of the different levels of interest that stakeholders may have in the evaluation, but still does not attempt to be all things to all men.

The second general consideration is to ensure that those stakeholders whose agendas are most likely to fall in line with the directions of evaluation recommendations also have the will and opportunity to take some action. What is particularly useful here is to obtain public commitments from senior managers in advance about taking positive action in the light of evaluation findings (this is normally used with the management development audit, see Chapter 9). Also, small advisory or steering groups which are set up at the beginning of a study in order to see it through to the implementation stage may provide some added backing to the actions that particular individuals need to take.

But stakeholders or evaluators also need to be in a position where they can make available sufficient resources to implement ideas and changes. This is so often overlooked, probably because it comes at the end of a long and unknown journey, but it is probably the single most important reason why so little comes out in evaluation studies. For example, recommendations suggesting changes in course material and structures on management programmes will require considerably more time commitment from tutors who are expected to implement the changes; proposals for new staffing or technical equipment in order to implement changes in management development systems will require considerable money; or proposals to change the philosophy of a course towards far greater self-direction must suppose that tutors have the necessary people skills to cope with the uncertainties involved. Furthermore, it is also worth taking into account some of the wider constraints on implementation, such as prior commitments, contracts held by individuals, and the wider effects of the organization's culture.

The discussion about the availability of resources raises yet a further question about the implementation of evaluations: is it clear that the assumed benefits from any particular change will outweigh the costs to be incurred in implementing such a change? The Gleicher formula (Beckhard and Harris, 1977, p. 25) is one way of considering this crucial question. In the inequality illustrated below:

$$[A \times B \times C < D]$$

D   stands for the total cost of resources to implement a particular change;

A   stands for the present system, or course, and what is seen to be *undesirable* about it;

B   stands for the new deal or proposals that are made, and what the apparent *benefits* of these might be;

C   stands for the *first steps* of action to be taken, the ease of taking these, and the clarity with which they are understood.

As a closing point to this section the Gleicher formula might serve as a reminder to aspiring report writers who will naturally be tempted to concentrate their attention on the desirability of particular changes being proposed. It draws attention to the fact that unless they can also convince people that there is something wrong with the present state *and* make positive suggestions about how to get started with a change, there is unlikely to be much of consequence resulting from their efforts.

Technicalities of interpretation and use of evaluation

The comments in this section are offered not as a substitute for the politics of evaluation (which are virtually inevitable), but as a way of reducing some of the unnecessary distractions that may be caused by political factors. Recognition of political issues provides no excuse for sloppy work, and it is still most important that evaluation work be carried out with a reasonable degree of technical competence, particularly if it is to be regarded with credibility by more disinterested observers. Two particular points will be considered in this section: first an overview of some of the ways of going about interpreting data, and second, the question of who should be involved in carrying out these interpretations.

Interpretation methods

There are two main distinctions in the way interpretation is carried out that are of relevance to evaluation issues. The first is the distinction between 'preordinate' and 'grounded' forms of analysis. The former are found most commonly in formal evaluation studies that use what have been labelled above as 'scientific' research methods. This means that the expected results of a particular study will be specified in precise terms beforehand as an hypothesis, and the type of evidence, or statistical significances that could lead to the support or rejection of this hypothesis are also specified (and in some extreme cases the whole lot is put into a bank vault before any data collection takes place as evidence of the researcher's integrity). Thus, in the example above of a course which received an average rating of 3.8, it might have been agreed beforehand that this would be considered a success if the mean rating was 3.7 or more, and no more than one rating was given below 3.0. This may be a rather trivial example, but it does indicate that the more the evaluator attempts to tie stakeholders down to criteria of success beforehand, the more the interpretation of the data will be driven by preordinate considerations. The main drawback of this is that many of the more interesting observations which could be made will be missed.

'Grounded' forms of interpretation are more appropriate in goal free evaluations, since classification categories of data are made only after the data has been collected. Also, the beginning and end of a study may not be so clearly defined since grounded forms of interpretation allow for several iterations in data collection, which can be used in later iterations to follow up on any of the interesting points and themes that have emerged in earlier surveys. Preordinate and grounded forms of interpretation have rather complementary strengths and weaknesses: the weakness of preordinate interpretation being that it necessarily restricts conclusions that might be drawn from the data; the weakness of grounded interpretations being that it may be very difficult to arrive at any firm conclusions at all from the data.

The second distinction is between 'logical' and 'creative' procedures for carrying out interpretations. Logical procedures are said to derive from processes in the left hemisphere of the brain (Mintzberg, 1976), and they involve working carefully through quantitative data and applying whatever statistical procedures are most acceptable. In the case of qualitative data, they require vigorous content analysis with classifications of categories often being made by several judges independently. Such procedures normally require full transcriptions of all interviews to be typed, answers to each question classified, coded, entered on to cards or computer records, and so on. Inevitably this can be an extremely time-consuming process, and it may bring the evaluator not much closer to having any notice taken of his or her results. Patton (1981) makes a strong bid for the increased use of more creative methods of interpretation and analysis. He also argues in his earlier book (1978) that the crucial gap between *knowledge* and *action* can only be bridged through creative thinking; and furthermore that this creativity can reside only in individuals. This is similar to what I have called the 'systems fallacy' earlier in this book, which points to the basic problem of attempting to deduce correct actions for the future based only on a knowledge of what has taken place in the past. Patton's (1981) book offers a wealth of suggestions about both creative data collection and interpretation procedures; one method that is quite helpful involves a 'total immersion' into data, interviews, transcripts, reports, and other relevant literature. This is then followed immediately by a 'workshop' approach with several individuals who have been involved with a particular evaluation discussing their impressions and attempting to put some order into the enormous diversity of observations and data. Simple brainstorming techniques can be very helpful for identifying issues and generating possible courses of action. The mental mapping process advocated by Buzan (1974) can then be used either to structure the analysis of issues or to identify key areas of action. Once again, one should make the point that such creative techniques are rarely completely self-sufficient. They are very useful for developing new ideas and perspectives, but it is still important to check out whether the evidence for these ideas really does exist within the set of data that has been collected. Reports and recommendations that are based entirely upon conjecture and hunches will have little claim to be taken seriously, even if they are creative.

Who interprets?

Then there is the question of who is to carry out the interpretation. The classic choice at this stage is between evaluators as 'experts' and stakeholders as clients, users, or decision makers. Although it is the evaluators who may have much more time available for this, it seems absolutely essential to involve stakeholders in the process if they are to have much ownership of the results. One way of doing this, which can be quite confronting, is to provide a comparison between what stakeholders and clients *said* was taking place in the organizational programme, and what the results of the evaluation indicate to be the real picture.

This does of course assume both that the evaluation is in the form which will lend itself to such a comparative presentation, and that there are sufficient discrepancies (or dissonances) for stakeholders to be forced to acknowledge that there is a problem and that something should be done about it.

There is another possibility here which may have particular relevance in the case of educational and developmental programmes, which is to go back to the people who provided the information in the first place, and to ask them what it *means*. This may require one or two iterations if there is sufficient time available, and the data represented for interpretation may be verbatim quotations (as Burgoyne and Hodgson, 1982, did with their protocol analysis technique), it may be presented in some condensed form, or interim summaries may be provided of the views of others in addition to that particular informant. There are some parallels between the latter suggestion and the Delphi Technique which is used for forecasting in that it may begin to produce some convergence of view of interpretation. It is an approach which is attractive, since it provides the potential to combine multiple perspectives on something which is bound to be multi-faceted; it enables interpretations of data to be made by people who have some direct experience of the phenomena from which the data are derived; and the procedure of iteration may also lead to considerable learning amongst those involved in providing interpretations, leading to far stronger backing for any changes that are indicated.

The role of the evaluator

Although involvement of stakeholders in interpretation and other decisions is highly desirable, if anything significant is to come from evaluation the role of the evaluator is still crucial. It also becomes more problematic if this is seen in increasingly political terms, as in this chapter. The two issues that require consideration are the effect of existing attitudes and beliefs held by the evaluator, and the problem of maintaining independence from sponsors despite rather close relationships with these people.

Almost by definition, an evaluator who is interested in matters of management training and development is likely to have fairly strong views about which procedures work, and about educational philosophies that are desirable, or undesirable. When one gets involved in evaluation it is hard not to end up liking some tutors, participants and other individuals, and disliking others. As with any other observer the evaluator is prone to develop contacts and information networks among people of like mind, which then may reinforce any prejudices or stereotypes that are already held. So what can be done about all of this? The answer lies in two parts: first in being aware of one's own biases and prejudices, and second in deliberately looking for information that might *falsify* one's pre-existing views.

The need to develop both links with sponsors and stakeholders provides a rather different threat to the integrity of the evaluator: it provides some danger of co-optation. But the requirement to try to bend the evaluation around the questions of various stakeholders does not mean that the answers to these questions should be in line with what the stakeholders want them to be. However, if the evaluator is in close contact with sponsors and stakeholders throughout, he or she is still likely to come under considerable pressure to produce the 'right' kind of report, particularly if there is a possibility of future funding being obtained from any of the stakeholders. One way of trying to maintain one's independence from such stakeholders is to ensure that the initial contract for the evaluation explicitly recognizes both the independence of the evaluator, and the possibility of negative (or indeterminate) results being obtained. This can provide a reasonable basis upon which to develop a working relationship, and thereafter the evaluator needs both the persistence and courage to keep the stakeholders involved.

Conclusion

To round off this chapter, and Part II of the book, it is worth offering some guidance on the choice of methods and designs according to the type of situation one is in. Four factors seem particularly relevant: the political context, the type of programme being investigated, the role of the evaluator, and the level of resourcing to support the activity. I shall consider each of these in turn in relation to the evaluation designs that they imply.

The political context

If the environment for training is essentially *supportive*, where the activity is seen as worthwhile by senior managers and other powerful stakeholders, it is much easier to adopt a design that interests tutors and participants, and hence work can be arranged for the purposes of improving and learning. On the other hand, as the environment becomes increasingly *hostile* with key stakeholders showing signs of scepticism which may well be reflected by participants, strategies should be adopted to answer the questions and doubts posed by these people, and to make efforts towards proving or controlling. However, in these circumstances it is also important to consider possible improvements that might be made. There is rarely smoke without fire; external criticisms may well be justified. An adequate defence against hostile external questions should not only demonstrate which criticisms are, or are not, justified; it should also show what positive steps will be taken to rectify problems that have been identified.

Type of programme

For the type of programme that is being considered, we can construct another two-dimensional matrix according to whether the activity is purely academic or is slanted towards application. We should also consider whether the underlying educational philosophy is didactic or based on discovery methods. On this latter dimension, programmes making strong use of lectures and programmed texts would appear at the didactic end, and those using action learning, experiential methods or projects would appear at the discovery end. Programmes employing case methods or simulations would come somewhere in the middle according to how they were handled in practice. Figure 6.2 provides some suggestions as to evaluation methods and approaches likely to be most appropriate in each case. It may also be used as a guide to whether to employ single or multiple methods in evaluation designs. With the more didactic programmes, objectives and goals can be clearly specified (whether or not they are really considered to be the right ones). At the other end it becomes much harder to agree on criteria against which judgements should be made.

This particular problem was tackled at the Center for Creative Leadership in North Carolina by Phillips (1990) in considering how to evaluate a developmental programme (which would be located in the bottom right quartile). Her conclusion was that one should design an element of complexity and uncertainty into the study by using multiple methods and looking for multiple possible effects.

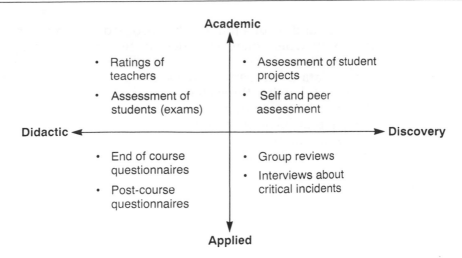

Figure 6.2 Methods by type of programme

The role of the evaluator

The key question here is whether the evaluator is an insider or an outsider in relation to the programme. If an insider, as when the tutor of some participants takes responsibility for evaluation, it is probable that these people will also be the main stakeholders for the evaluation. If this is the case, then it is most important that feedback be obtained from all participants. Methods should be simple, and might involve a mixture of quantitative and qualitative methods. When the evaluator is from outside the organization, feedback will be much more public; careful preparation is therefore needed to ensure that all influential stakeholders understand and support what is taking place. Care will also have to be exercised to ensure that their views and questions are taken into account.

An intermediate position occurs when the evaluation is being done by someone in the same organization, but outside the training function. Here, perhaps the best approach is for the evaluator to adopt a discreet monitoring role based on standardized but limited reporting arrangements, with the option of more detailed investigation if necessary.

Resource availability

The link to the previous factor is that when resources are limited there is no option but to carry out evaluation work for oneself; where they are more generous it is possible to fund work to be carried out by outsiders.

Clearly the methods used must adapt to the means available. When resources are limited then data will be gathered and used within existing constraints by relying on short questionnaires, end-of-course reviews, and results that can be absorbed within normal tutor meetings. It is only when there is generous funding, or cheap labour (student projects!?), available, that it is possible to conduct in-depth interviews, obtain data from many sources and produce formal reports.

In the following three chapters I shall elaborate further on the choices that may be made under different circumstances, using real evaluation studies that have been conducted over the last few years. These illustrate some more of the practical problems that can be encountered, and the need for flexibility and creativity when conducting evaluation.

PART III

Applications: Evaluating methods, courses and policies

Introduction to Part III

Previous chapters of this book have discussed both the theory and practice of evaluation across a wide range of contexts. Although specific examples have been drawn from particular contexts, or settings, there has been no deliberate attempt to discuss what is unique about the problem and approaches in one setting or another. This approach has been pursued because, as was explained at the beginning of the book, one of the main aims here is to bring together and, it is hoped, synthesize some of the distinctive approaches that have been adopted in different settings in the past.

Now the time has come to concentrate again on the different settings in which evaluation may take place, using, where appropriate, the ideas developed in earlier chapters. In particular, I shall examine the kinds of questions and problems that typically occur in different settings, and the methods or approaches that are usually adopted in tackling them. In each case I shall provide a few brief examples to illustrate these points.

This part of the book is divided into four chapters, each of the first three considers evaluation at a particular *level* and the fourth looks to the future. For this purpose a simplified version of Burgoyne's 'hierarchy of decisions' will be used (Burgoyne and Singh, 1977), and the levels chosen will be those that I find easiest to distinguish between: (i) methods; (ii) courses, programmes and systems; and (iii) policy. Within each of these three levels we shall discuss how the practicalities of evaluation vary from setting to setting. The three settings to be considered will be those outlined at the beginning of this book:

1   The 'educational' setting which covers management courses held in business schools and colleges, and which would normally lead to some kind of qualification.
2   The 'training' setting which would cover most of the activities of management training centres and many of the post-experience programmes in educational establishments.
3   The 'development' setting which refers to in-company schemes such as performance review, career development, job rotation, and other arrangements intended to develop managers, where there is not an explicit training or educational content involved.

7 Level 1: Evaluating methods

Management education and training

At the level of *methods* there does not seem to be a very great difference between the settings of education and training, since in the management field, at least, most methods seem to be widely disseminated into both settings. As one might expect, the evaluation of education and training methods is largely the preserve of psychologists and professional educators or trainers. In some cases there is also a little interest from managers, particularly when it concerns a controversial method that some of them may have had some experience of – such as T-groups – but even then the interest seems to be at an anecdotal level. The main question considered about such methods is how well they work, and what is their effect. This effect is normally assumed to be some kind of learning, or attitude change; but occasionally, as in the case of T-groups, a great deal of attention has been directed to determining whether or not the effect is a harmful one. There are a few examples of people attempting to understand *why* such effects take place, but these are definitely in the minority of published studies.

One of the most comprehensive reviews of evaluation studies at this level is provided by Rogers, Cooper and Burgoyne (1977). From this it is clear that the 'scientific' design has predominated with an emphasis on measurements of participants' state both before and after the use of the method in question. Comparative studies where two or more matched groups are assigned to two or more different training methods are also very popular and Rogers, Cooper and Burgoyne make a strong bid for their continued use in the future.

One of the most valuable studies of an educational method has been provided by Bligh (1971) in relation to *lecturing*. He reviews almost 100 experiments that had been carried out to compare the effectiveness of lecturing with other teaching methods, the majority of these being based on tests and measures conducted before and after a particular session took place. Bligh's conclusions, which are based mainly on adding up the number of studies that pronounce for or against lecturing, were that:

1   with the possible exception of programmed learning the lecture is as effective as any other method for transmitting information but not more effective;
2   most lectures are not as effective as more active methods for the promotion of thought; and
3   changing student attitudes should not normally be the major objective of a lecture.

(Bligh, 1971, p. 4.)

Interestingly enough, Bligh also supplies evidence which suggests that there are consistent differences in the effectiveness of individual lecturers, although for reasons that may be obvious, such questions have received rather less attention from researchers than the more detached investigations into the value of the method *per se*.

Another comparative study is provided by Partridge and Scully (1979). This was a particularly careful study which looked at the relative merits of the case method and a business game in teaching business policy at an introductory level. A class of thirty-eight students was divided into eight small groups which were matched in terms of academic attainment up to that stage in their course. Four of the groups participated in a business game which lasted for twenty hours of the normal undergraduate course, and the other four groups used a series of case studies for a similar period of time. All students involved in the experiment completed a business policy test on two occasions: the first occasion being immediately before the start of the experiment, and the second occasion being twelve weeks later (and four weeks after the end of the case/game sessions). Answers to the business policy test (see Figure 7.1) were accessed anonymously by a judge who was also asked to make direct comparisons between pairs of 'before' and 'after' questions without knowing which was which. The results of the 'before' and 'after' test obtained by Partridge and Scully are given in Figure 7.2 and based on these results it was possible for them to show, at a significance level of 95 per cent, that the game groups had improved over the test period more than had the case groups.

The above example is part of a continuing debate between proponents of 'case' and 'gaming' methods, and this one clearly came out in favour of the latter. However, as Rogers, Cooper and Burgoyne (1977) point out, the evidence in support of the superiority of gaming

---

Business Policy Test

Demonstrate your knowledge of the following concepts and their ramifications by explaining their meaning and providing examples of their application in a business enterprise setting.

1 The time dimension is a strategic factor in most business decisions.

2 The organization's decision makers should be aware of the relationships of measurable variables, i.e. they must determine not only the levels or rates of change but the best direction of movement in view of probable developments.

3 Management must develop the ability to collect and abstract relevant decision-making information from the environment.

4 The organization's strategy must carefully balance long- and short-run considerations.

5 Decisions made today partially create the environment faced by the organization in the future.

6 Plans or policies are carried out by a series of consistent decisions that vary in accordance with variances in the environment.

7 Functional decisions within the firm are interrelated and should be kept in dynamic balance.

8 Management must constantly reappraise its company's strategy in the light of new challenges and opportunities posed by its internal and external environment.

9 The firm operates within any number of constraints which may be personal, economic, physical, technological, or social in nature.

Figure 7.1 Business policy test (from Partridge and Scully, 1979)

Groups	% Improvement
Game Group 1	22.98
Game Group 2	24.82
Game Group 3	34.93
Game Group 4	27.58
GAME TOTAL	27.58
Case Group 1	22.06
Case Group 2	22.06
Case Group 3	11.49
Case Group 4	5.76
CASE TOTAL	16.09

Figure 7.2 Results of 'before and after' test (from Partridge and Scully, 1979)

is somewhat thin, and the majority of research findings are overwhelmingly negative in relation to the knowledge of facts provided by games.

This leads to the observation that cases and games are likely to have rather distinctive strengths and weaknesses, and therefore comparative evaluations based on single measurement instruments are unlikely to be able to provide a fair overview of such strengths and weaknesses. It also suggests that what takes place within a game or case study is also rather more complex than might be inferred from the design of an evaluative study. One obvious area of complex variability is in the role of the tutor/lecturer in each case. Partridge and Scully attempted to control for this factor by removing the teacher from any involvement with the business game and by making his participation in the case study series as neutral as possible. The problem with this is that it makes the results, although scientifically tidier, of rather limited relevance to 'real' examples of cases and games being taught actively by teachers. However, these results may have greater use in the future when one considers the growth of 'distance learning' methods which may attempt to dispense with immediate contact with the teacher.

Another limitation of scientific studies, which are aimed at *proving* the value of a particular method (of which Partridge and Scully's study is a well executed example), is that even if it is possible to demonstrate with consistency the superiority of one method over another, it is still very difficult to explain with the research design of that kind *why* the superiority should be there. Nor are such studies able to provide any insight into the problems of particular methods, and offer suggestions about how these might be overcome.

One study that *did* attempt to look at the internal workings of the case method is reported by Argyris (1980), and (*pace* Partridge and Scully) one of his major observations was to do with the crucial importance of the role of the teacher in conducting the class discussion around a particular case study. The purpose of this study would probably be classified as *improving* and therefore, characteristically, Argyris was concentrating on the kind (rather than the amount) of learning taking place, and on the processes in the classroom which apparently contributed to this learning.

The Argyris methodology included his attendance at a three-week executive programme for top managers based on case studies taught by star performers. These were drawn from leading American business schools such as Harvard, Virginia, Standford and Yale. First, Argyris interviewed all the faculty members involved with this programme about how they used the case method and what they tried to achieve within classroom discussions. These 'espoused theories', as Argyris called them, included some consensus on the point that cases (in real life) are really incomplete, and therefore that there really are no right or wrong answers to case studies, and also that it is necessary to keep the dependence of participants on the faculty members down to a minimum. An analysis was then carried out of the actual interactions taking place in classroom discussions. By counting the number of comments or questions that one student directed to another, compared to the number of questions or comments made by members of the faculty to students, it was possible to construct an index of student independence – on the assumption that more student communications taking place indicated higher independence. Similarly, the absolute number of questions asked, or statements made, by the faculty member within a session was taken to serve as an 'index of the control' exerted by the faculty member on that session.

Results of the analysis showed that the students were not particularly independent (over twice as many comments being made by faculty members as by students), and that faculty members did seem to exert a fairly high degree of control in most cases. The one exception to this was when one faculty member, having controlled interactions at the beginning, allowed rather more student responses in the remainder of the session. Further interviews with faculty members revealed that one of their methods for maintaining control of the session was to prepare beforehand a very comprehensive analysis of the case and a list of questions which (they believed) were essential to understand what was going on. One of the games then played (largely unconsciously from the faculty's point of view) was for the faculty member to offer small portions of his or her 'right' solution progressively as the session developed. Students then became very expert at detecting hints and cues which might help them to uncover the 'right' solution from the faculty member.

This seemed to be one of the processes which enabled these outstanding case method teachers to use what is supposed to be a student-centred teaching method in a highly directive way. And Argyris used this to support his view at a wider level that such teaching methods will in practice encourage 'single-loop' learning (learning to correct errors within a given set of operating assumptions or principles), rather than 'double-loop' learning (becoming able to question the basic principles and philosophies within which one is normally operating).

The significance of the Argyris study in evaluation terms is that it can lead to an understanding of why certain outcomes do or do not take place, even though in terms of the discussion in Chapter 3, his primary focus upon the *processes* taking place within the programme. There was, of course, no direct comparison between the case method and other approaches in this instance, so it would not be possible to conclude that the case method has any superiority over lectures, business games, or other methods; but, through linking the observations into a specific theory of learning, it should be possible to compare it indirectly with other teaching methods.

A recent study by Armitage (1993) into the educational benefits of simulations was based on experiences of MBA students in the UK, France and Holland. Data was collected by interview and questionnaire concentrating on context and processes. Results showed that most students found this to be a valuable supplement to other learning methods on the MBA, and was particularly useful for seeing how theory can be put into practice. It was also evident that student learning was affected by the role of the tutor and the extent to which the simulation design employed principles from experiential learning theory.

By way of conclusion to this section, despite the preponderance of studies adopting scientific methodology emphasizing outcomes, pre-tests, and post-tests, I must confess a preference for the more construct-ivist approach exemplified by Argyris and Armitage which is concerned with the *processes* of a particular method being used in practice. It seems to me that the insights obtained from a single study carefully conducted along these lines are considerably more convincing than a weight of statistical evidence obtained from a series of scientific studies. This brings to mind the comment from Peters and Waterman (1982), referred to in the previous chapter, that people tend to be far more influenced by stories which are sufficiently complete to make sense by themselves, than by data which is by definition utterly abstract.

Management development

As mentioned earlier, within this category fall the activities and proce-dures for developing managers which normally take place *inside* the organization, and which do not have the appearance of courses or educational programmes. This, therefore, covers procedures for select-ing managers, for assessing and appraising individual performance, schemes for providing them with a wide job experience at an early age, or schemes to develop the effectiveness with which groups of managers can work together. Once again, the people with interest in the evalu-ation of management development methods are personnel and manage-ment development specialists, and there is a reasonably strong psycho-logical bias in much of the work that has been done.

One area which has received considerable attention is that of *selection* procedures – partly due to its obvious importance for organizations but also, perhaps, because there are relatively simple criteria to determine how successful a particular technique has been. For example, for a given group of, say, 100 managers, it is possible to compare the number who would have been selected or rejected on a given test with the number who were subsequently successful or unsuccessful in their jobs.

Figure 7.3 indicates the number of managers who would have been successful or unsuccessful in a company where 40 per cent of managers were subsequently successful, and if a particular selection test been administered which, at random, would have accepted 30 per cent of managers and rejected 70 per cent of them. In this case only twelve out of thirty managers would have been selected (i.e. 40 per cent would have been successful). Figure 7.4 shows the hypothetical results based on a slightly more effective selection procedure from which it can be seen that, although still only 40 per cent of the managerial population are successful, of those who would have been selected by the procedure some twenty (i.e. 67 per cent) would have been successful. And the

Selection decision	Subsequent performance		Total
	Successful	Unsuccessful	
Accepted	12	18	30
Rejected	28	42	70
Total	40	60	100

Figure 7.3   Result by chance

Selection decision	Subsequent performance		Total
	Successful	Unsuccessful	
Accepted	20	10	30
Rejected	20	50	70
Total	40	60	100

Figure 7.4   A 'good' result

Selection decision	Subsequent performance		Total
	Successful	Unsuccessful	
Accepted	25	5	30
Rejected	15	55	70
Total	40	60	100

Figure 7.5   An even better result

results in Figure 7.5, indicating an 83 per cent success rate, imply an even more effective selection procedure . . . or so the theory goes.

Unfortunately there are some very real constraints on the possibilities of assessing the validity of particular selection procedures, such as the need for management to make use of the data in personal decisions and thus creating a self-fulfilling prophecy. The above examples (Figures 7.3 to 7.5) assume that no decisions have been taken in the light of selection test results; but the pressures on management to make use of such information in real life seem almost overwhelming. For example, Stewart and Stewart (1981a) conducted an extensive review of research into 'assessment centres' but were able to identify only one example of an evaluation study which had not 'contaminated' itself by feeding information to management during the whole test period involved. This isolated example was carried out by Bray (1966) who tested some 355 young managers, and then followed their progress for the next eight years. The results of the study showed very high association between the predictions of the assessment programme and the level in the organization achieved by these managers by the end of the eighth year. This result was particularly significant since Bray had kept all of the individual results from the assessment programme secret; but, unfortunately, despite the high degree of 'uncontamination', Stewart and

Stewart (1981a) were still able to point to a number of methodological flaws in this study which reduced the overall significance of its findings.

The problem with this type of evaluation research is that when even the best studies, such as the one just described, are flawed in any way, the case for assessment centres over other selection procedures, such as interviewing or straightforward psychological tests, remains unproven. As Stewart and Stewart comment:

> There remains doubt because it seems difficult to produce a really watertight experimental design which will permit uncontaminated data to be compared over a considerable length of time with job related measures of performance.
>
> (Stewart and Stewart, 1981a, p. 216.)

The difficulties of avoiding contamination, and of providing adequate control for outside influences are particularly evident when attempting to *prove* the value of particular in-company management development methods. The results from the use of assessment centres in selection decisions, are most equivocal even though this should be one of the easiest methods upon which to generate definitive evidence. Consequently, much of the other evaluation work conducted in this area is of a rather more 'pragmatic' flavour. Two further examples should suffice.

Firstly, the conduct of appraisal interviews has long been recognized as one of the critical areas in the successful functioning of appraisal systems. Just how this is known to be a problematic area is not entirely clear but it seems to be one of those accepted 'facts' based upon direct and reported experiences. In the area of appraisal interviewing most attention has gone into *improving* the ability of managers to conduct successful appraisal interviews. Once again this does not appear to have been based on significant investigations into the processes and effects of actual appraisal interviews; most ideas about how to improve skills in appraisal interviewing have been drawn from other areas of research pursued by social and occupational psychologists. From these areas of research have been derived general principles about the way appraisals should be conducted in different circumstances, and these have been incorporated into training programmes aimed at developing the appropriate skills. Thus, in some respects, an evaluation problem to do with in-company management development has been translated automatically into a management training solution without a very great knowledge of the processes that are supposed to be being changed.

The second example is about the evaluation of methods in the general area of organization development and team building. Although there has often been a considerable interest in the *outcomes* of such methods, this has normally been directed towards the purpose of *proving* their value, or otherwise. There are two main reasons for this: firstly, the area of organization development is particularly diffuse and varied with regard both to the methods employed and to the targets of those methods. Thus the difficulty of establishing a clear criterion against which to measure the value of any particular intervention is far greater than in the case of something like assessment centres and, therefore, this area is not seen as particularly fruitful by those who would use their scientific methods in the service of evaluation. Secondly, there is a sense in which technology is at odds with the central values of organization development, particularly amongst those who would seek to reassert its potential as a radical force for change (Reynolds, 1979). Published examples of studies purporting to demonstrate the value of organizational development have tended to be one-off case studies, often written by people who played a major part in the interventions themselves (Blake *et al.*, 1964).

In some respects, the tendency of organization development (OD) practitioners to evaluate their own work is more than crude self-promotion. When an OD intervention is underway and the importance of group work and openness of feelings and perceptions is being stressed, it is exceedingly difficult for outside observers to maintain their detachment without being sucked into the processes that they are supposed to be observing. I was made very much aware of this point when observing a group of managers as part of an evaluation study. A major portion of the discussion in one session centred on the managers' perceptions of myself and a colleague as evaluators, and about our feelings as visitors to a group which was discussing us as if we were not there. When the purpose of evaluation shifts more towards *improving* or *learning*, the possibility of clear distinctions being maintained between evaluators and participants becomes increasingly slim. In these circumstances there is a strong case for adopting the 'co-researcher' role: where tutors, researchers and participants attempt jointly to understand the processes and outcomes associated with their joint endeavours.

Conclusion

Thus, attempts to evaluate development methods may fail to satisfy the purist, and much of this stems from the diffuseness of the target that is being examined and the difficulty of isolating procedures from the real constraints and politics of the organizations in which they are taking place. Moreover, much of the effort that has been devoted to *proving* the value of techniques in this area may well have limited value in the long run. A greater potential seems to exist for purposes of *improving* and *learning*, and perhaps this gives recognition to the significance of values and commitment in this area – which is therefore not amenable to dispassionate and analytic description.

8 Level 2: Evaluating courses, programmes and systems

Courses, programmes and systems imply a higher level of complexity than mere 'methods' in that they are normally built up from combinations of methods, often employed over a significant period of time. But in another respect they are more *specific* to the context to which they are employed, and therefore any finding and ideas developed about such courses, and so on, are likely to be less easily generalized to other contexts, than are findings about methods. This might point to a rather more pragmatic approach towards evaluation at this level, and we shall be able to examine in some detail in the following sections whether this prediction is correct. Because of the context-specificity at this level, it also makes sense to deal with each of the three contexts of management education, training, and development separately in this chapter.

Management education

The overriding question about most educational courses and programmes is how good they are in academic terms. This question is asked by various validating bodies such as university senates in the UK, the *Conférence des Grandes Ecoles* in France, or in the USA the American Association of Collegiate Schools of Business (AACSB), and so on. It is the price that must be paid if these bodies are to set their seals of approval behind such courses, and therefore make them viable products in the competitive world of management education. The greatest scrutiny normally takes place when a new course is being proposed.

Proposers must be able to demonstrate that the syllabus conforms to that prescribed by the body in question; that the appropriate number of contact hours will be achieved in each area; that assessment procedures will be able to demonstrate without ambiguity that students have attained the appropriate levels; that the institution can provide sufficient facilities and resources to mount the programme; that the staff likely to be teaching the programme have sufficient levels of experience and qualifications, and so on.

These are, largely, bureaucratic details which are extracted before the course is actually run in order to guarantee reasonable conformity and uniformity across that particular part of the educational system. The validation procedure tends to be considerably more rigorous in the USA than in the UK, and as a general principle it becomes less rigorous the further one moves up the ladder of educational qualifications. Therefore in the UK, for the time being, there are only preliminary moves to prescribe any form of syllabus, whereas reasonably detailed syllabuses are required for taught master's courses at universities; and the required detail increases for undergraduate courses at higher education institutions that are externally validated.

Once the relevant validating body has pronounced the design of the educational product as satisfactory, the teachers concerned with the course are then left reasonably free to get on and run it. The validating bodies take very little interest in evaluating such programmes (either with respect to outcomes or the processes on the courses) and the question of quality control is left to external examiners, who may occasionally be asked to submit reports on the course to the validating body. This has been tightened up in recent years, partly to forestall Government criticisms of educational quality, and the duties and reports of external examiners are now taken very seriously by institutions. Recent increases in the levels of competition between institutions for students have resulted in greater import being attached to teaching performance. When this is translated into a major criterion for promotion, teachers have become more interested in providing evidence of teaching quality.

Despite these changes there is still much external incentive for teachers to take a very great interest in evaluation of their own courses. For the institutions there is always the danger of creating unwelcome publicity; additionally, for individual teachers there have been few rewards either for good teaching or for taking additional interest in the teaching process. Nevertheless, there are still some hardy souls who persist with being interested in educational processes, and therefore the *subsidiary* questions that may be asked about educational courses and programmes are often phrased: how enjoyable; how valuable; or how well taught a particular course has been. In such cases students are normally asked to provide a significant amount of the information, and occasionally they take a more active role in initiating structured evaluation procedures – approximating to what has been described as 'consumer evaluation' in Chapter 5.

I intend to provide three brief examples of course evaluations; these will mainly be in the area of student feedback, often initiated by the teachers involved. It seems difficult to find an example of evaluation carried out by a validating body, at least in the sense that I have been using the word 'evaluation' up to this point. In passing, however, I might offer some gratuitous advice about course submission to validating bodies. Four points here are:

1   Provide sufficient details of the course and syllabus, but ensure that this is expressed clearly and simply.
2   Be extremely careful to ensure that the rubrics, structures, and logic of assessment are correct.
3   Make sure that any external examiners involved are seen as respectable.
4   Go and talk in advance to the officials who will be involved in vetting the proposal if you feel there are any unusual features involved (such as self-directed learning, peer assessment etc.).

The first genuine example of course evaluation comes from a fairly typical example of a student feedback questionnaire used by the New York University and, as can be seen from some of the sample questions in Figure 8.1, it is based entirely on multiple choice responses. These questionnaires are filled in anonymously by students at the end of each semester and are collated and analysed by the administration. It should be clear from the sampled questions that this instrument is basically concerned with *proving* and with forming judgements about the quality of each teacher's performance. The results of these questionnaires are not normally made public although they are said to be used in decisions about promotions and awarding tenure to members of the faculty. There is, however, a little scepticism about just how much notice is taken of this kind of information in actual decisions, since some of the more senior professors in the university are reputed to receive consistently low ratings from this instrument. Not only is there some doubt therefore about whether this instrument is really used for *proving* except perhaps in a few exceptional cases where evidence needs to be brought against people; but it is also of limited value in indicating to the teacher how he or she might actually *improve* teaching performance.

Of slightly more use, particularly since they are intended for teaching development, are some of the feedback questionnaires employed in British universities. The example given in Figure 8.2 is taken from questionnaires used at the former North-East London Polytechnic. This uses relatively simple Likert-type questions which concentrate on what the lecturer seems to be doing and how he or she handles the relationship with students on the course. In this questionnaire there is no attempt to provide a judgement of the lecturer's overall performance;

---

1 Would you recommend this instructor to a friend?

Yes	1
Yes, with reservations	2
Neutral	3
No, with reservations	4
No	5

2 Give this course a grade (independent of how you feel about the instructor):

A	B	C	D	E
1	2	3	4	5

3 Give this instructor a grade (independent of how you feel about the course):

A	B	C	D	E
1	2	3	4	5

All things considered, how would you rate each of the following compared with all *other* courses and instructors you have had:

	Bottom 10%	Next 20%	Middle 40%	Next 20%	Top 10%
4 Amount learned	1	2	3	4	5
5 Instructor	1	2	3	4	5

How is your instructor in class?

	Yes	Unsure	No
6 Provides useful examples	1	2	3
7 Thought provoking	1	2	3
8 Clear	1	2	3
9 Enthusiastic	1	2	3
10 Constructive	1	2	3

Figure 8.1 Sample questions from a student feedback questionnaire used in New York University

but the data provided by students of their experience of different aspects of the course should provide the lecturer with some pointers about the areas that might most constructively be worked upon should he or she wish to make some improvements.

A third example is from a number of studies that have been carried out in the Department of Management Learning, Lancaster University, with a view to improving the quality of some of the postgraduate courses being offered. One approach is to ask students, especially if they already have some knowledge of evaluation procedures, to conduct their own evaluation; for example, the questionnaire illustrated in Figure 8.3 was produced by a sub-group of students, and circulated to all other members of the course towards the end of a diploma programme. It was specifically designed to produce some quick and easily absorbed evidence about the effect of this programme on the students (i.e. *proving*), and the open-ended comments produced by that group in response to the questionnaire are illustrated in Figure 8.4.

Students carrying out evaluations of courses may find it of use to

The Lecturer:	Strongly disagree	Disagree	Neither agree nor disagree	Agree	Strongly agree
1 Is clear and understandable in his or her explanations	1	2	3	4	5
2 Stimulates students to think independently	1	2	3	4	5
3 Makes a genuine effort to get students involved in discussion	1	2	3	4	5
4 Makes good use of handouts e.g. duplicated lecture notes, examples of problems, reading lists	1	2	3	4	5
5 Makes constructive and helpful comments on written work	1	2	3	4	5
6 Gives a good factual cover of the subject matter	1	2	3	4	5
7 Writes legibly on the blackboard	1	2	3	4	5
8 Is readily accessible to students outside formal classes	1	2	3	4	5
9 Tries to link lecture material to laboratory work/practical work/seminars	1	2	3	4	5
10 Can be clearly heard	1	2	3	4	5

Figure 8.2   NELP Student feedback questions

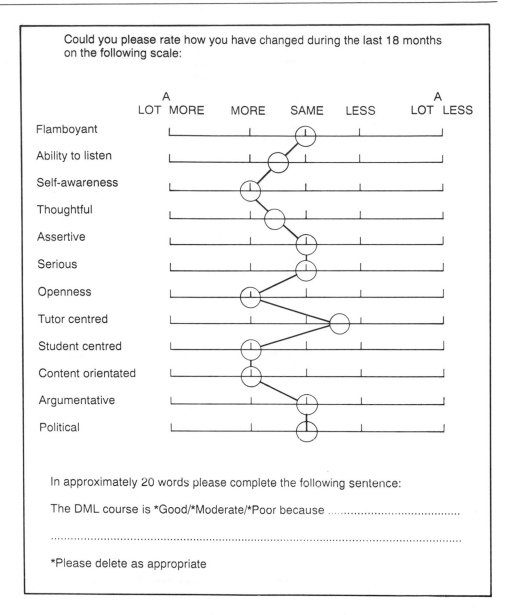

Figure 8.3 Questionnaire (and mean ratings)

reflect upon how much, and what, they have derived from the course; they also seem interested in comparing such outcomes for themselves with those of their colleagues on the course. Since, in most cases, they will be very unlikely to follow the same course again, they may be somewhat less interested in evaluative questions directed to *improving* future courses. That is why it is often easier for evaluations of educational programmes aimed at *improving* to be conducted by staff of the institutions concerned, but preferably not by the tutors and lecturers

Rating	Comment
Good	'I have been made to re-examine my existing values and practices and to test my ideas out in the "real world".'
Good	'I feel different.'
Moderate	'The tutor team still suffers from tensions as yet unresolved or even clearly identified. This split has re-created itself in the community. We lack synergy.'
Good	'It has made me aware of new issues and has made me re-think some of my long-held views and prejudices, without necessarily making me change them.'
Unrated	'I have only had to attend one module of it.'
Good	'Because it allows for individual development due to its (generally) loose-structured nature.'
Poor	'Having examined current issues around a constructivist/student centred perspective, they put you through the "exam" mincer and slap a pass/fail mark on you.'
Unrated	'You meet such interesting people in congenial surroundings to discuss matters of vital importance and consuming significance some of the time.'
Good	'It has updated my knowledge of teaching in a large number of important areas.'
Good	'Because it's challenging and you meet monks.'
Good	'It gives a broad base of knowledge, skill and experience in the esential areas of management learning that is of value to me both as a learner and a teacher.'
Good	'It brings together industrial trainers and management teachers, and seems able to accommodate the "Georges" and the "Berts", the "James" and the "Brians".'
Good	'It attempts to develop individuals in a variety of ways from where they are.'
(13 returns out of 14 distributed)	

Figure 8.4 Open-ended comments from questionnaire shown in Figure 8.3

who may have gained their commitment to early models of the course. We have therefore found that the most useful evaluations aimed at this purpose are conducted along constructivist lines, and by an insider not directly involved with that particular course. Open-ended questionnaires or interviews seem to work best where they concentrate on questions such as:

- What did you like/dislike most about this course?
- What aspects of the course did you find most helpful/less helpful in contributing to your learning?
- What advice would you give to new students joining this course next year about how they can ensure that they are making the most of their opportunities?
- What are the three most important changes that could be made to this course in order to make it better in the future?

Although it is sometimes possible for tutors to talk over these matters with students, there may be some inhibitions on either side if the tutor has been closely involved in teaching on the course. Therefore, it does seem easier for a relative outsider to take this role, and also to take responsibility for collating results, extracting themes and issues, and providing feedback of overall results and conclusions to all those who participated in the study. Studies carried out at Lancaster University on the postgraduate research programme have highlighted the need to provide more effective support between students (thus resulting in the establishment in a network of research sets); and occasional difficulties encountered in relationships between students and supervisors have resulted in closer monitoring of supervisor/student relationships in general. These are a couple of improvements that have been made to the postgraduate research programme as a result of evaluation studies; other changes have been made in the case of several of the Department of Management Learning's other programmes in order to deal with different issues and problems identified in this way.

Management training

The main interest here concerns the extent to which training courses can actually be used by those who attend them, and whether they are of relevance to the needs of these individuals, or to the needs of the organizations that have sponsored them. This contrasts somewhat with the interest in maintaining academic standards and quality which has predominated in the context of educational courses and programmes – but perhaps it should still be noted that both maintain a primary focus on *outcomes*.

Evaluations of these programmes are conducted or initiated by the institution itself, since most training establishments are slightly more independent from outside control and validation than are educational institutions. (Here I am referring to *educational* rather than *financial* controls.) But in most cases it is not at all clear what purpose is to be served by such evaluations, and there seems to be a large element of 'ritual' in the case of management training.

One of the most common rituals is the short (two page) questionnaire which is distributed at the end of a course, and sometimes at key points during the course. The questionnaires may be open or closed. Of the two, closed formats are rather more common when used in the middle of a course because they take less time to complete and can provide clear indications of ups and downs in the course, more-or-less as they are happening. The focus of such questionnaires is *inputs*; and with end-of-course questionnaires there are usually a few items to cover administrative aspects. These questionnaires are often known as 'reactions sheets' or 'happiness sheets'. An example of a fairly typical end-of-course 'reactions sheet' is given in Figure 8.5.

End of Course Evaluation								
Name of	Coverage of subject				Usefulness			
Lecturer:	Poor	Satis.	Good	Excel.	Low	Moderate	High	Very high
1	1	2	3	4	1	2	3	4
2	1	2	3	4	1	2	3	4
3	1	2	3	4	1	2	3	4
4	1	2	3	4	1	2	3	4

		Low	Moderate	High	Very high
1	Quality of accommodation	1	2	3	4
6	Quality of restaurant	1	2	3	4
7	Quality of administration	1	2	3	4
8	Overall rating of value of this course	1	2	3	4

Figure 8.5 'Reactions sheet' distributed at end of a training course

The purpose of this type of evaluation may not be immediately transparent. The questionnaire illustrated in Figure 8.5 might be thought of as aimed at *proving*, but this is not really the case, since the results produced are rarely taken as anything more than diagnostic. Provided that the ratings are reasonably high in comparison with similar programmes (as was discussed in Chapter 6), no action needs to be taken. If any of them drop below what is considered to be an acceptable level, this may indicate that some remedial action is necessary, such as changing the course or the teacher involved. In this respect, therefore, the real purpose of such routine evaluation (especially when it is used during a course) may in way be regarded as *improving*.

Practice in leading business schools

At the Lyon Graduate School of Business in France the *Département de Méthodes et Moyens Pédagogiques* has been developing a range of educational and evaluation methods for different circumstances and audiences. For example, for short courses a questionnaire using a mix of closed and opened items and focusing on the main inputs is normally adopted (see Figure 8.6 for translated extracts); with a course that aims to develop managers' skills at working in groups, evaluation concentrates on the process aspects with an emphasis on contributing to participant *learning* (see Figure 8.7).

Q4. Can you assess the programme according to the following objectives:				
Objectives	**Completely achieved**	**Largely achieved**	**Partly achieved**	**Not achieved at all**
Broadening your skills in new areas				
Deepening existing skills				
A better understanding of your job				
Other (explain with comments):				

Q9. Which topics in this programme:		
were covered too much?	were covered insufficiently?	should be added?

Figure 8.6   Extracts from short course questionnaire at ESC Lyon

At Ashridge Management College programmes are run which last for one or two weeks. A relatively conventional design divides the day into slots of 1½ hours, with each topic (and tutor) lasting for one or more slots. In these cases evaluation normally takes the form of a four or five page questionnaire at the end of the week requesting 'happiness' ratings supplemented by optional comments for all of the sessions, plus a few questions about the housekeeping aspects of the course. These are seen by tutors as part of the ritual of course closure and there is some cynicism about their usefulness. But a number of more interesting experiments have been tried in recent years. These include mapping participant reactions throughout a programme in order to understand how different parts of the educational process contribute to learning.

The tutor:	**Yes**	**No**	**Why**
12 obtained agreement from everyone about how to proceed			
14 listened and allowed everyone to explain themselves			
16 was not judgemental about ideas proposed			

And finally:

- In what respects do you think the group was working well, and why?

- Note any problems or incidents encountered which were not fully dealt with.

- What observations do you have on the techniques of 'facilitation' which were exhibited?

Figure 8.7   Extracts from evaluation questionnaire on group development programme at ESC Lyon

This is part of a more general attempt to move the dominant philosophy from that of a teaching institution to a learning institution. Other courses which have a developmental focus tend to employ more ongoing reviews and to use open-ended questionnaires that start by inquiring into the learning objectives of the individual participant.

A final example from Ashridge is an action learning programme for chief executives which was evaluated by Ian Cunningham when a visiting Fellow at the College. In keeping with the learner-centred philosophy of action learning, this study was based almost entirely on interviews conducted at the workplace or during group (set) meetings. The final report made extensive use of quotations to enable the managers to speak 'with their own voices'. Thus, it is clear that methods can, and should, vary within any one institution according to the nature of programmes that are being covered. Although it will also be evident that some methods, such as the latter example, are more time-consuming and expensive than others. This, as I have indicated at the end of Chapter 6, is an important factor to take into account when considering evaluation designs.

At the Henley Management College evaluation practices also vary across the wide range of programmes. One interesting evaluation variation is the executive development workshop which makes considerable use of self-diagnostic instruments. Managers and their bosses rate themselves on a wide range of skills or competences before the course and these ratings are used as part of the workshop agenda. The evaluation emphasis is on the individual and on his or her work *context*. As described earlier in the book, the aim of such emphasis is to contribute directly to the learning process.

From time to time, institutions decide to conduct 'in-depth' studies of a particular course or programme; these often require considerable resourcing, often from outside experts. Since additional funding is normally involved the studies tend to have far higher visibility than routine evaluation work, and therefore it is almost inevitable that they will be drawn into the political arena. Such political implications may relate to the reasons for commissioning a study in the first place – to the kinds of questions that different people would like to have answered, or to the kinds of answers they would like to receive to those questions. Two examples of such studies will be presented below, before offering some recent examples showing how these problems can be tackled.

Example 1: Keeping track of the client

This first example is a study of a junior management course carried out for the staff college of an important public sector organization in the UK, and which was conducted by myself and two colleagues on a part-time basis over about four months. The main question asked of us was whether we considered this particular course to be meeting the current and future needs of the business, and whether there were changes that could be made to the course in order to strengthen its relevance. Behind this question we were also aware from other sources in the company that top management had been asking some pointed questions about the value of the staff college, and there was therefore the possibility of significant reorganizations being introduced in the near future. Nevertheless, in the meantime our clients were the senior tutorial staff in the college itself.

The remit given to us by the clients suggested that our primary focus should be on the organizational *context* from which managers attending the course had come – rather than on inputs and processes within the course itself. We therefore started talking to samples of managers, both those attending the current course and some who had attended similar courses several months previously about the nature of their jobs, what they found difficult about those jobs, what they felt were the keys to successful performance in them, what changes they were experiencing at the present time, and what kind of changes they anticipated in their areas of the business in the near future. Some of these talks (or interviews, if one wishes to be pedantic) were tape recorded, but the majority were recorded by the interviewer in note form, with direct quotations being taken down whenever they seemed to be of significance.

One particular interest of ours in this study was to examine the perceptions of change in the business held by managers who had attended the course, and compare these with perceptions of change from managers who had not attended the course. A content analysis of the several dozen interviews conducted indicated that those managers who had attended the course were perceiving more of the broad changes taking place in the business, than those who had not attended. However, those managers who attended the course did have considerable difficulty relating their perceptions of what was going on in their own *immediate* work environment to the material that was introduced on the course. This was indicated by the fact that there was no difference in perceptions at this level, between those who had, and those who had not, attended the course. One of the principles in the 'transfer' of training is that managers should be able to relate materials on the course to contexts where each manager has some degree of control, and in this respect the course did not seem to be succeeding. Consequently one of our main recommendations was about ways of 'grounding' the material and content of the course in the experiences of individual managers through making use of methods such as projects, individualized case studies, and action learning sets.

Another problem was a fundamental flaw in our design: we had been asked to look at whether the *course* was meeting the needs of the business, but we were asked specifically not to observe any of the course sessions in practice. We therefore had to make do with second-hand information about the process of formal sessions on each course which was provided by participants and tutors. The need to piece together indirect evidence occasionally placed us in a rather insecure position and, although we were eventually reasonably confident that we knew what it was that we had not observed, the absence of direct access did create an additional problem.

The results of this study were delivered in a form which was closest to the predominant culture of the company, and they were presented on time! The only additional problem by this stage was that both of the vital clients who had been instrumental in commissioning the study had been moved on to new jobs elsewhere in the company. Although these individuals had formally been replaced, the main commitment that had been generated for making use of the results was therefore lost. Many of our recommendations were also superseded by a significant reorganization of the training function which followed soon after, and we were only able to hope that some of them had been quietly assimilated into the new arrangements.

Example 2: Multiple stakeholders

The above example may be taken as a cautionary tale about the importance of maintaining good links with vital clients and sponsors during an evaluation study when one is an outsider. Above all, one should try to discourage clients from being moved or reorganized during the period of the study.

This second example also encountered some problems with clients, although these were less drastic, and it was therefore possible to accommodate them adequately within the aims of the study. Another interesting feature was the necessity to change the evaluation design quite significantly as the study progressed; the earlier part being close to the experimental research school of thought, and the latter part adopting much more of an interventionalist model. The course which was the subject of the evaluation was run on a part-time basis over a period of twelve months for a group of training officers from an Industrial Training Board. The training board sponsored the participants and the course was run by Durham University Business School.

The main question posed at the outset by the programme director (who also commissioned the evaluation study) was whether the course had any effect on the way the training officers went about their jobs. Therefore a short multiple-choice questionnaire was administered before the start of the programme to all prospective participants, including some who did not eventually come on the course. The questionnaire (see Figure 8.8) was intended to measure how they currently saw their jobs, and their attitudes towards the work involved in these jobs. These questionnaires were complemented by two types of repertory grid, the

---

(A) My job involves me in:

		Not at all	Somewhat	Quite a lot	Extensively	Very extensively
1	The actual training of employees in the group	1	2	3	4	5
2	Encouraging managers to make their own decisions about training without my assistance	1	2	3	4	5
3	Concentrating on giving advice to companies at a training *policy* level	1	2	3	4	5

(B) Please circle the number that best expresses your view on the continuous scales below

9	I find it easy to get managers to make their own decisions about training	1 2 3 4 5 6 7	I find it difficult to get managers to make their own decisions about training
10	There are a few constraints in this job	1 2 3 4 5 6 7	There are a great many constraints in this job
11	This is the type of job that suits me very well	1 2 3 4 5 6 7	This job does not suit me very well

Figure 8.8 Extracts from questionnaire used before and after training officers' course

first using a set of elements such as 'Myself as I am', 'A Progressive Manager', 'An Effective Trainer', and so on from which about six constructs were derived using the normal triading method (see Chapter 5); the second type of grid asked the training officers to define a set of elements based on what they experienced as the main problems in their jobs. They were further asked to provide a set of constructs which expressed how they typically tried to cope with each of these problems (for further details, see Easterby-Smith, 1977).

Some of the information, especially that provided by the latter of the two repertory grids, was provided to the course director before the programme started in order to help him adapt the content and design to the needs of the group that he was likely to be encountering.

After this initial burst of data collecting activity, I maintained a low profile in this course, occasionally visiting it while residential sessions were being held, and chatting informally to participants in the bar, but not attending any of the formal sessions. Brief 'Reactions Sheets' were distributed by the course director at the end of each module, and these were collected and collated by himself and a secretary. My next major involvement with the programme began about one month before the final week, when I telephoned the course director to discuss arrangements for the final phase of data collection, and for the presentation of evaluation results at the final review meeting. During this conversation he mentioned to me that the manager in the training board who had been given liaison responsibility for this programme was coming under some internal pressure, and that he would be most interested to know a little more about how the programme was going. It was at this point that the evaluation study began to change from the experimental research to the interventionalist 'school of thought'.

I telephoned the manager concerned, to tell him how things were going, and at the same time I decided to ask him about the kind of information that he was hoping the evaluation might produce. His immediate response was that he hoped that it would 'break through the fogs about what it is that the training officers say they are getting out of this programme'. He also added that perhaps I should ask his other colleagues in the training board, who had nominated individual training officers from their areas to come on this course, what they were expecting their nominees to get from the course, and to what extent they felt this had been achieved. This I agreed to do.

There are three main aspects of this development. Firstly, by asking the manager what *he* was expecting from the evaluation, I was acknowledging that the course director (who was paying for the study) was not the sole client for the evaluation. Other people clearly felt they had a stake in it, and it therefore became necessary to try to accommodate their needs too. Secondly, by accepting a wider definition of the client group, I was being influenced to look for things other than those specified in the formal aims of the course, or in the original design of evaluation. The third aspect was that I was thereby starting to become involved in the politics of the training board. The manager with liaison responsibility was evidently coming under some pressure from his colleagues to justify expenditure on this programme. Perhaps one way of countering some of this pressure was to send an 'evaluator' around to them to ask precisely what they expected their own training officers to obtain from the course – and these were questions which the manager knew his colleagues would have difficulty in answering.

I had now committed myself to spend additional time travelling around the country meeting managers in various areas of the board's operation. Due to the deeper involvement with the sponsoring organization, my interviews with participants towards the end of the programme were considerably broader than simply asking them to complete the pre-course instruments once again (although this was conscientiously done in each case).

As a result of these broader interviews it was possible to identify a number of particular issues which had had an important impact upon the way this particular course ran, and some of which would have a bearing upon the designs of subsequent courses. Some resulting issues were:

1   Senior management appeared to be exceedingly unclear about why they were sponsoring this programme, and what they believed the training officers should be getting out of it.
2   The initial meetings of participants in small groups with the course director and evaluator before the course began were experienced by some as 'traumatic'. They commented that in discussions with the course director they felt they were being sold a product and that they would virtually have no opportunity to influence what went into the programme; they also disliked being asked to complete the pre-course evaluation instruments (although no one refused openly to do so).
3   Some parts of the programme were regarded as markedly less successful than others, and an important factor in this was the degree of commitment that each tutor appeared to be making to the course.
4   The 'project' part of the course was crucial to the success for each participant. If the choice of project was a 'good' one the overall experience was positive; but if the project turned out to be unsuccessful, this rather soured the experience of the whole course.

In the discussion at the end of the course about the evaluation report, it was the description of some of the issues arising which created by far the most interest. Not only did it provide answers to some of the questions that people had asked, it also enabled them to recognize some of their own contributions to understanding what had taken place. The more quantitative results of the attitude surveys and repertory grids were noted, but they did not create much interest, partly because they were addressed to questions which were only of marginal interest to those involved (*proving*), and partly because they had been manipulated statistically in order to provide conclusions. Since participants and others could not see clearly the link between the information they had provided and the conclusions that were drawn from that information, this material therefore had relatively low face validity.

Recent studies that tackle stakeholder and observational problems

Two major issues emerge from the above examples concerning the importance of using data-collection methods that get as close as possible to the subject of interest, and the need to deal very carefully with the range of interests and perspectives represented by different stake-holders.

Whenever conducting an evaluation nowadays I insist on being able to observe, and if possible to participate informally, in key parts of the course or programme. The value of this was brought home to a colleague, Morgan Tanton, and myself when observing a senior executive programme run at a leading business school in France. Although many of the sessions were very interesting, others were rather boring, and participants would complain extensively amongst themselves about some of the less stimulating lecturers. However, when the final evaluation sheets were completed it was hard to see much difference in the ratings between sessions for which the informal comments had been conspicuously positive or negative. If anything there was a positive gloss put on almost all of the ratings. When a group of participants were confronted about the discrepancy between their informal comments and their written ratings with regard to one of the tutors, they explained that they didn't see the point in rating him down because he was a pleasant person and they thought the data would be used against him.

The moral of this is to be aware not only that evaluation procedures may have different purposes, but that most of the actors involved will have their own views about what those purposes are – and this may well influence their response to any questions posed.

One study I conducted with a colleague in the UK, for the Department of Social Security (DSS), investigated further the uses that different stakeholders may have for evaluation data (Easterby-Smith and Mackness, 1991). The study was being conducted as part of a national training programme for managers in nearly 1,000 local DSS offices that were about to have new computer systems installed. This was a very large capital investment and some £60 million was allocated to train staff in the use of the new system. Given the scale of such an investment the reputations of a number of senior managers were linked with the success, or otherwise, of the training programme. It was, therefore, very important to ensure that the programme achieved its objectives – and certainly that it could not be used as a scapegoat if things went wrong elsewhere with the new computer system. Accordingly, a central evaluation team was established to monitor the hundreds of five-day courses run in different regions of the country.

Our role was to advise this central team on the design and operation of the evaluation procedure. The methods involved a mixture of brief 'happiness sheets' with rating scales and space for a few written comments from which data were collated and compared month by month and region by region, plus occasional observational visits to courses and follow-up interviews by telephone. Each month a report was produced which was circulated to key stakeholders. After this had all been running for several months we conducted some additional interviews with stakeholders to see how they had been using the data thus provided and whether it supplemented any other forms of information they might have about how things were going. The results of these interviews are summarized in Figure 8.9.

STAKEHOLDERS	HOW EVALUATION DATA/PROCESS USED
Regional Directors	• Skimmed statistical results before passing them down the line. • Occasionally jotted comments and suggestions in margins of report. • Ideas for change came from direct contact with trainers and trainees.
Trainers	• Not interested in statistical results. • Liked written comments from trainees because they 'put the meat on the bones'. • Ideas for change came from discussion with trainees and raw questionnaires, not from evaluation reports.
Trainees	• Disliked doing quantitative ratings. • Enjoyed writing comments because it gave a chance to reflect on what they had got from the course.

Figure 8.9 Use of evaluation data by stakeholders

Figure 8.9 shows how different stakeholders will use information according to their particular needs: the senior managers were interested in information that might be used, in the *proving* sense, as a performance indicator in comparison with other regions; the trainers were interested in anything that helped them assess progress of the programme and how it might be *improved*; and the trainees were largely interested in whether it would contribute to their own *learning*.

Management development

In this section I shall try to cover both the organization-wide systems aimed primarily at the development of an *individual* manager, and the programmes or interventions which are ostensibly aimed at improving the functioning of groups, or the organization as a whole. As far as evaluation is concerned, much of the work in these areas has been of a pragmatic nature with an emphasis on *improving*, although, particularly in the case of OD, there have been a number of rather traditional research studies aimed at *proving* the value of an intervention. Where evaluation has been carried out, this has been assumed to be primarily for the benefit of personnel specialists and senior management, although there are examples of wider client groups being acknowledged, especially when the democratic values of an OD intervention managed to be translated into the practice of its evaluation. I shall start by discussing the evaluation of OD interventions, before returning to a consideration of systems aimed primarily at the development of *individuals*.

Methodologically there are two distinct traditions in OD. Firstly, there are a number of case studies of single interventions which in most cases have been written by the consultants who managed those interventions. Apart from the obvious commercial advantages for consultants who are able to publish 'respectable' evidence of the success of their own interventions, there is also a strong tradition of action research in this area which leads rather naturally to such self-evaluations. This action research often forms a crucial part of an OD intervention, and usually involves some form of data collection in the organization, feedback of that data to a wide range of interested parties, and some form of resultant action planning. Action research generally works better when the managers, who are themselves the objects of the study, also participate quite extensively in carrying out the study; hence the tendency noted above for client groups to become quite wide in a number of instances. French and Bell summarize these two traditions neatly in relation to action research:

> Two philosophical and pragmatic values underlie action research. The first value is that action plans and programmes designed to solve real problems should be based on valid public data generated collaboratively by clients and consultants. This belief calls for action to be based on diagnostic research – *and action should follow research* . . . The second value is that action in the real world should be accompanied by research on that action so that we can build up an accumulative body of knowledge and theory of the effects of various action directed to solving a real world problem – a *research should follow action* mode of thinking.
>
> (French and Bell, 1978, p. 98.)

The second tradition in OD is markedly different in function, and the emphasis on accumulation of knowledge tends to lead to distinct methods being employed also. Frequently these take the form of traditional research methods employing multiple-choice questionnaires to survey large numbers of managers and employees in order to identify whether changes have taken place across the organization as a result of OD interventions or the operation of management development systems. This survey data is often backed up by statistics on organizational performance (such as absenteeism, sales figures, customer complaints, and so on), and occasionally by interview data. However, it is rare to find the subjects of such surveys involved in interpreting survey results – as they might well do in the first tradition.

One of the reasons for the diversity of evaluation practice is the complexity of conducting work in this area. At least five problems can be noted.

Firstly, it is by no means easy to agree on the conceptual boundaries of what is to be investigated. There is enormous variation in the practice of management and organization development, and each contains a wide variety of philosophies, value systems, techniques, and structures. Secondly, there are practical problems of defining boundaries when evaluating techniques and procedures that supposedly cover complete organizations. This may not be too difficult in an organization, or sub-unit, employing a few hundred people; but it poses severe limitations when the organization employs several hundred thousand people. For example, a survey of cultural values in a large multinational company, eventually obtained a response sample from 116,000 employees (Hofstede, 1980). (Analysis of this enormous amount of data was helped not a little by the technology of the company in question!) Thirdly, evaluation of programmes and systems frequently has implications for the politics of the organization. People's jobs and careers may be closely linked to the success or failure of the management development programmes that they are promoting or sponsoring. Since the information produced by the evaluation can be a very potent political weapon it may well be used to support the views and interests of those who control its dissemination. A fourth reason for difficulties in this area, especially when aiming to *prove* something, is that if organization-wide changes are supposed to be generated, then these can be very difficult to demonstrate, and as we noted from the discussion in Chapter 2, there may be very little agreement indeed about what constitutes the *right* changes. Fifthly, when OD methods are being used, it may be exceedingly difficult to distinguish between actions undertaken as part of the intervention, and research conducted as part of the evaluation. As in the hallowed tradition of the Hawthorne study (Mayo, 1946), both action and evaluation may have significant, and unpredictable effects on their subjects.

There is an enormous range of published literature about OD, including numerous evaluation studies which have attempted to assess whether or not it works. French and Bell (1978) cite a number of papers, each of which reviews the results of dozens of individual studies. But which, collectively, do not lead to any definitive conclusion. But it is worth emphasizing a couple of points made by French and Bell with regard to these evaluation studies. Firstly, they note (up to 1978) a trend towards more tightly controlled and comparative research designs which make use of independent evaluators, a trend they are strongly in support of. Secondly, they regard the scarcity of acceptable theory –

about how and why OD works or does not work – as a major hindrance to the establishment of definitive results about the effects of OD. My comment on this, from an evaluation perspective, is that there may be a contradiction between French and Bell's two points, and perhaps they would have done better to have concentrated on *processes* with a view to *improving* OD, before returning to the quest for *proof* with its concern with *outcomes*.

At the level of systems for development of individuals one of the most extensive examples of the evaluation is known as the management development audit (Easterby-Smith, Braiden and Ashton, 1980). It is, on the surface, intended to provide information about how well management development systems are working in practice. The core of the audit procedure consists of a selection of short questionnaire modules (Figure 8.10) each about different forms of management development that might exist in the company being investigated. The modules cover subjects such as appraisal systems, career development systems (or career development when there is no system in existence), training, general comments on organizational climate, and so on. These modules are selected by the person conducting the audit (normally after pilot interviews and discussions with top managers), according to what is supposed to exist in the company. The questionnaires are largely of a multiple-choice format; they are completed by a sample of, or by all managers in the organization; and the results are normally collated and

---

Y1 Have you been given an appraisal within the last 3 years? (Within this organization)

Yes   1
No   2

Y2 The time which has elapsed since your last appraisal is:

Less than 12 months   1
12 months or longer   2

Y3 At your last appraisal: (please answer all sections)

		Yes	No	Don't know
(a)	Were specific training recommendations made?	1	2	3
(b)	Were personal targets set for the future?	1	2	3
(c)	Was your performance for the last year graded?	1	2	3

Y4 Who keeps a copy of your appraisal?

		Yes	No	Don't know
(a)	Yourself	1	2	3
(b)	Your immediate superior	1	2	3
(c)	Personnel department	1	2	3

Figure 8.10 Part of 'appraisal module' from a management development audit questionnaire

tabulated by computer to show variations in response by level and function of the organization. The analysed results also provide indices of organizational climate which can be used to monitor the effect of subsequent changes, and opportunities for managers to say how useful they consider the existence of different parts of the management development system to be.

These points may lead to the impression that the audit is really designed for *proving* the effects of management development (and senior managers are often not disabused of this when an initial agreement is being sought to go ahead with an audit). But underneath this there is a fairly strong agenda, and process, aimed at *improving*. This is how it works. Before the major survey part of the audit is initiated, interviews are carried out with a sample of senior managers (normally including the chief executive) about how they think the management development systems are actually working in practice, and about what their ideal schemes would look like. These two viewpoints may be described respectively as the 'formal' and 'normative' views of management development. It is then possible to compare both of these with the 'perceptions' of what is actually taking place as provided by managers who are on the receiving end. This has been described as:

> Although most senior managers will already be aware of how management development works, comparison between formal and perceptual views afforded by the Audit . . . enables them to base their decisions on reliable information. Comparison assists in deciding what is to be changed – whether it be the actual development activities or the formal statements of intentions that are made.
>
> (Easterby-Smith, Braiden and Ashton, 1980, p. 7.)

There are many other ways in which the data generated by an audit can be used to facilitate changes, although this inevitably depends upon the imagination of the evaluator (auditor), upon his or her own power base, upon the degree of support provided by sponsors and other senior managers. The point here being, as emphasized in Chapter 6, that the value of conducting an audit is dependent more upon the political skills of the auditor than on his or her 'technical' expertize.

Inevitably there are a few drawbacks to the audit procedure. Firstly, in completing an audit it is rarely possible to cut corners and the minimum amount of work that must be undertaken is really quite substantial. Secondly, it is based on some fairly explicit ideas of systems theory (which in view of the five typical problems discussed above is one way of handling both conceptual complexity and organizational size). The use of a systems framework means that it is possible to draw additional conclusions from questionnaire results – such as why there is so rarely any genuine linkage between the appraisal sub-system and the training sub-system. Points such as these can be highlighted quite easily with this framework. Nevertheless, it must be recognized that there is a tendency for 'systems' forms of analysis to beget 'systems' forms of solutions to problems. Some people may feel that this is a very good thing, and yet there is a significant body of opinion which considers that systems solutions are not necessarily appropriate in modern (and the more successful) organizations (Peters and Waterman, 1982).

Finally, it should be noted that the management development audit is a relatively recent idea, and most studies, although internally comparative, have only taken snapshots at one point in time – or at least within a very limited period. When looking at organizations as a whole it is normal to allow several years to lapse before any significant changes in views, attitudes, or climate might reasonably be expected. Consequently there are only a small handful of follow-up studies that have been conducted in the same organization aimed at monitoring the effect of changes introduced after an earlier audit, and the results of these studies have not yet been made publicly available. Hence it will be a little longer before the full potential of the management development audit can be assessed in perspective.

Conclusion

One factor that should be apparent from the discussion in this chapter is just how value-laden is most evaluation practice. In a way this is hardly surprising; but in another way it may emphasize the inadequacy of views that concentrate on evaluation as a purely technical process.

This relates to the function of 'ritual' so frequently provided by evaluation in the area of management training. One of the features of rituals is that there is often a major difference between what appears on the surface to be happening and the deeper meaning of the actions involved. In the case of evaluation this is reflected in the difference between the overt and covert purposes to be served – and one example of this is the management development audit.

The likelihood of there being covert purposes when conducting evaluations at this level suggests the importance of adopting an interventionalist style, and I think this is largely unavoidable if evaluators wish to have any genuine influence within organizational contexts. The main danger of adopting this style is fairly obvious: that the evaluation activity will become compromised and will lose the credibility which can derive from its supposed detachment. That is not necessarily an argument for desisting; but it is an argument for being alert to the implications of the choices one must make as an evaluator.

9 Level 3: Evaluating policies

There is a degree of mystique about policy formulation: it is the kind of thing that is done by *senior* people; organizations that do not have policies often seem to get into trouble; and policies are generally considered to be 'a good thing'. The way I shall use the term 'policy' here is simply as being indicative of consistencies in the nature of certain decisions, actions, or activities. In theory, policies come before the actions and decisions to which they relate, although in practice it is very often the other way round. The evaluation of management education and development policies involves examining patterns of decisions, actions or activities within the context of institutions and organizations, but often at a national or super-national level.

Management education

Of the three contexts to be discussed in this chapter, management *education* invites consideration at the most macro level. Policies for management education are very frequently the concern of national governments, or of powerful national foundations, associations, or institutions. With this in mind it is often very difficult to separate policy issues from the interests of individuals, groups, or political organizations.

The questions that may be asked of management education at a policy level therefore tend to vary according to the interests of those who are doing the questioning. Thus national governments, which frequently tend to be in the funding role, are likely to be concerned with issues of cost-effectiveness. At its crudest level this may be measured by the number of diplomas, MBAs, or PhDs produced, for every pound or dollar pumped into the education system. A second group of crucial stakeholders for management education, are the organizations which are likely to become the future employers of business graduates, and which also provide the managers who attend shorter post-experience programmes within the educational system. Here the primary concerns, or questions, are likely to be about relevance: whether the skills and abilities supposedly learnt within educational institutions are really likely to contribute to the overall effectiveness of the employing organization – does it really contribute to the 'bottom line'? For the third major group of stakeholders, the educational institutions, the policy questions are likely to centre on the best mix and range of programmes or activities which will contribute to *their* reputation, prestige, and financial viability.

Evaluation methods at this policy level tend to be surprisingly 'constructivist' (especially in the UK). The normal practice is to employ consultants, or to establish working parties and commissions to solicit opinions from a sample of reliable observers or informants. There are two reasons for this. Firstly, one is clearly dealing with questions on such a wide scale that unless they can be narrowed down very precisely, there are so many intervening variables that a more 'scientific' approach simply could not cope. Secondly, at this level it is quite pointless trying to disguise the political nature of decisions being made, and therefore it seems quite acceptable to use overtly the kind of information that most senior decision makers really rely on – informed opinions (or, as the former University Grants Committee in the UK used to acknowledge openly, informed *prejudice*), from people whom they trust and respect.

There have been a number of critiques of management education produced both in the USA and the UK, by authors with wide experience of the respective systems, but without the adoption of any very clear evaluation methodology such as making an attempt to identify a reasonably balanced sample of 'informed' observers (Livingston, 1971; Hayes and Abernathy, 1980; Mant, 1969). In the UK, the classic evaluation of management education was jointly commissioned by the British Institute of Management and the Confederation of British Industry in 1970, and published in 1971 as the Owen Report. This investigation was prompted by concerns from major industrial organizations (which had provided a substantial part of the initial funding of the first business schools created in the UK during the early 1960s) that the business schools had moved into providing highly academic forms of management education (MBAs and PhDs), rather than the more practical and skills-orientated education that was assumed to be of greater relevance to British industry. The investigators, led by Trevor Owen, formerly a personnel director of ICI, visited fifty-three firms in manufacturing industry and talked to senior managers both in personnel and operating functions. The report, and its conclusions, were based on a consensus of 'considered opinion' from those people surveyed. Predictably, the report confirmed many of the existing criticisms of management education in the UK up to that time: there was too much emphasis on academic courses; the selection of students for those courses was based on academic criteria rather than potential managerial ability; and graduates from courses usually had an inflated view of their own abilities, assuming that they were already just a short step from the managing director's seat. Given the sample from which these views were solicited, the conclusions of the Owen Report were not surprising, but they were influential; and that is the way of much evaluation at this level.

Similar investigations have been carried out in the USA. Debate on the appropriate nature and direction of management education culminated in an investigation sponsored by the American Assembly of Collegiate Schools of Business (AACSB). The investigation was conducted by senior professors from two leading business schools and included over 500 interviews and 10,000 questionnaires completed by stakeholders. Publication of the study (Porter and McKibbin, 1988) showed problems in a number of areas. It was felt that the curriculum should be broadened to include more of the 'soft' subjects, such as interpersonal skills and leadership, and should pay much more attention to international aspects. There was also a certain amount of criticism from industry about research work on the grounds that most academic research, with the possible exception of some developments in finance, is largely irrelevant to the needs of industry. However, most business schools who contributed to the survey felt pleased with their achievements over the last twenty years (numbers on MBA courses had increased by a factor of twenty over this period), and most alumni who responded were extremely satisfied with the system of which they were products. Well, they would say that, wouldn't they! And this is one of the difficulties in policy-oriented studies. The people who are likely to know most about a particular topic are also those who will have a vested interest in maintaining the *status quo*, or at least in limiting change. There was little attempt in the Porter and McKibbin study to question seriously the underlying values of business education in the USA: that it is dominated by MBA programmes; that most students pass through business schools before they have had any significant work experience; that schools distrust direct collaboration with industry because it might prejudice their objectivity (although they are happy enough to take sponsorship from industry); and that academic research, and hence careers, should be devoted to producing largely quantitative research for publication in obscure journals. Not only were the people who conducted the study insiders, but so too were most of the people who were consulted (and this includes the American corporations which are staffed, especially at senior levels, by alumni from prestigious business schools).

A number of parallel studies have been carried out in the UK, for example Handy *et al.* (1987) and Constable and McCormick (1987), and further studies have taken place in the USA, too (GMAC, 1990). The distinctive feature of these UK studies is that although they were conducted largely by academics, they were initiated by industrial and government interests, and for this reason they were able to be rather more confrontational about current practice and provision. In cases where evaluation studies are controlled by committees the membership is clearly of great importance. In the case of a recent national review of MBA programmes in former UK polytechnics the chairman described how carefully the members of the panel were chosen to reflect different interest groups – including people from industry, from the polytechnic sector and other educational sectors, and independent advisers from outside the system. He commented:

> In practice there was remarkably little disagreement about the core of the report and our recommendations . . . The key seems to have been getting an appropriate group of people together with a brief to produce a report on a specific topic. (Lock, 1992)

The above studies gathered opinions on management education and MBAs from people with relevant experience and opinions. There have not been many studies that have taken a strictly scientific research design, although it is worth describing one such study which took place in the 1970s because of its ambitious scale and the fact that it can illustrate many of the points that I have been making about the problems of experimental approaches to evaluation. The European Foundation for Management Development commissioned a study which was intended to identify, scientifically, the effect of MBAs provided by leading business schools in a number of different European countries. The basic design required both monitoring a complete year's intake to the MBA programmes in eight institutions in six different countries and following the progress of those students over a period of two years. A very extensive battery of psychometric measures and questionnaires was assembled and administered to all students at the beginning of their courses, and these were repeated (on rather smaller samples of *available* students) at the end of a period of one year. An attempt was also made to obtain matched control groups for all of the students by asking each one on the MBA programme to nominate a friend of his or hers who was not on the programme, but who was similar in ability, personality, and general career progress. This led to one rather interesting result, as we shall see in a moment.

Measures for this evaluation were chosen largely on the basis of their known reliability (that is, they were known to be accurate measures of traits such as achievement motivation, or numerical intelligence), rather than because they were thought to be highly appropriate to the skills and attributes that MBAs were supposed to be generating in those students. This choice of measures led to one extraordinary incident (which perhaps illustrates some of the pitfalls of highly quantitative evaluation designs) when the results of the 16-PF (personality) tests were being compared between a number of institutions in different countries. A working group had been making considerable progress over a day and a half in producing some interesting interpretations of the difference exhibited between English and Italian students . . . until one of the researchers suddenly realized that the scoring protocol for the 16-PFs completed by the Italian students was based on the English version of the test, which used both a different language *and* structure. Therefore, this working group had spent over a day developing what they thought were very meaningful interpretations from data which were shown to be completely random.

That is the first cautionary tale from this particular study; the second, that results failed to demonstrate any positive (and significant) effect from the MBA programmes. Hence, a decision was taken not to publish any of the reports from the working party. The one unpublished manuscript that has come into my possession was based on the data gathered at Manchester Business School. This part of the survey was unable to identify any significance differences in a sample of MBA students over the one year period of study; but more seriously, it found that the MBA students indicated rather less adjustment (as measured by McClelland's TAT, the 16-PF, and the Gough adjectival test) than the control group who were not attending the MBA, but who for the most part were working in industry. Perhaps this provides, at last, some more quantitative (and inside) evidence to support the views expressed in the Owen Report. But then, that is how things were in the 1970s, and to be fair, most of the MBA programmes have changed very significantly since those days.

Management training

In order to make sense of current training provision in the UK it is important to recognize the effect of early national arrangements on its evolution. Thus, in the period from 1965 to 1985 national policy was dominated by the Industrial Training Boards, the Training Services Agency, and the Manpower Services Commission. However, none of these was set up primarily to service the needs of *management* training, and the extent to which they have taken any interest in this area has been a result of the initiatives and pressures of concerned individuals and groups. Also, the emphasis has changed somewhat over time as political and economic pressures have changed. For example, the Manpower Services Commission was set up in the mid-1970s to co-ordinate national policy on employment and on industrial training (largely at a supervisory/operative level). At that time the main interests in management training were in the areas of updating skills for managers, thus providing greater mobility in the workforce, and in stimulating within companies the roles of management training and management development advisers. This latter aspect probably derived from the fact that many of the industrial training boards had invested a considerable amount of resources over the years in such advisory roles. However, as unemployment became more and more of a political issue in the UK, the priorities regarding management training shifted towards the provision of courses for redundant executives, and towards a range of initiatives intended to create new successful small businesses.

In the latter part of the 1980s the agenda changed again. As mentioned above, the Management Charter Initiative (MCI) was set up in the wake of the Handy and Constable reports. This national body comprising government, suppliers and industrial clients was established to co-ordinate policy towards management education in the UK. This had become necessary in response to a number of factors including very rapid growth in MBA programmes, strong and increasing demand at undergraduate level, a whole range of new collaborative programmes being established between companies and business schools, and threatening noises from the government about the possibilities of privatizing postgraduate management education. MCI working parties tackled a number of problems in the sector. These included the immediate shortage of competent management teachers (which led indirectly to the establishment of the highly regarded Management Teaching Fellowship Scheme funded by the Economic and Social Research Council); the need for government to provide adequate infrastructure if business schools were to be able to move towards independence from state funding; and the need for companies to play their part in a new order by committing themselves to codes of good practice.

As with most policy-oriented bodies, the working parties were filled by the 'good and the great', and energy was directed to, (what were seen at the time as) the main issues of the day. There is always a tendency in these cases for current rationality and scenarios to dominate thinking (for example the overriding assumption of continuing linear, or exponential, growth in demand for management education which was held in 1988 has already been found, by 1992, to be wrong – most of the growth has stopped, and in some areas has gone into reverse). This is not to decry the achievements of MCI. It has done much to raise awareness of both the issues and potential of management education, but some of its initiatives have been overtaken by the emergence of new bodies (such as the National Council for Vocational Qualifications – NCVQ – which happens to have much more funding behind it) and some of its ideas (such as requiring all managers to become professionally chartered) simply did not gain sufficient support to be worth implementing. The key point here, however, is that when dealing with national policy issues there is often a very thin line between the impact of supposedly independent evaluation data and the reality of financial and political muscle.

At the level of individual companies and organizations, the policy issues have less obvious political impact, although the range of debate and questions are rather more diverse. As is the case with national policy, at a company level policy issues are also largely the concern of those at the top – in this case, top managers, directors of training establishments, and senior personnel managers. Burgoyne (1981) provides an interesting overview of many of the theoretical issues that may be involved in consideration of management development policies within companies. In practical terms some of the questions that may be asked and which reflect on company training policy are:

- Should management training be run within the company, or contracted out to other organizations, or scrapped altogether?
- *If* management training is to be run within companies should this be set up as a profit centre which charges commercial rates to all participants or as a cost centre which is effectively subsidized by the company's central financial resources?
- Should such a management training college be staffed by line managers on secondment, or by 'professional' trainers, or by a mixture of both?
- Should management training be provided for distinct strata in the organization, thus reinforcing the identity of different levels, or should it concentrate on particular skills or topics, thus perhaps reinforcing the notion of a 'task' culture?

There are other policy issues regarding *how* management training should be conducted and organized. For example, should an emphasis be placed upon providing training *away* from the job, or should this be integrated as closely as possible with the manager's normal job (as can be the case with action learning approaches)? Another major dilemma for management training policies, particularly during periods of rapid environmental change, is whether management training should be attempting to *push* new ideas and approaches on managers, or whether it should take a more low-key role of supporting the *status quo* and simply responding to initiatives for change which emerge from the top of the organization.

I am dubious about the contribution evaluation can make to debates at either the national or the company level, if it is seen in terms of *proving*. Many of the policy issues with respect to management training are both political and value-laden, and it is unlikely that evaluation studies would be of sufficient scale or sufficiently targeted to provide a definitive contribution to such debates. Rather, it seems that the best role for evaluation to play in these cases is one of *improving* the quality of the debate through concentrating on, and illuminating, key issues instead of trying to take the policy decisions out of the arena of political debate.

One example of this form of evaluation is provided by the report of the Institute of Manpower Studies, Sussex University, into the operation of the Youth Training Scheme (YTS) (Hayes *et al.*, 1983). One of the main themes of this report, which was based on extensive interviewing with both providers and 'clients' of YTS schemes, was to identify 'skill ownership'. If managers are being trained at the public expense should they themselves be seen as the rightful owners of the skills that they obtain from the training (therefore entitled to use them in any way they feel fit), or should they have some obligation to use them to contribute either to employing organizations or to the communities in which they live? Furthermore, should training programmes have an obligation to concentrate on skills that may be of use in one context or another?

In this way the evaluation study was able to contribute to the debate by examining the dilemmas that underlie specific policy decisions. And, furthermore, such a study could also contribute to achieving some consensus over the criteria against which such training programmes might be judged subsequently – although no doubt in the time-honoured way of collecting informed opinions from reliable observers/participants!

Even then it may be difficult to avoid the political arena, as Richard Thorpe and Ardha Best found when they were commissioned in 1989 to investigate the reasons for high dropout rates on the Employment Training Scheme (a successor to YTS). They felt that a qualitative methodology was most appropriate in this case, so proceeded to interview a sample of trainees to determine the reasons for dropping out. The results of these interviews showed much dissatisfaction among trainees – about the inflexibility of training provision, poor quality of some courses, and continued uncertainty about whether the training would actually lead to any permanent employment. However, when the results of the study were presented to representatives of the sponsoring body it was clear that they were already aware of most of the issues raised; there were few surprises and the data seemed to confirm what was already known. Much to the surprise of Thorpe and Best some of the more critical passages of their report were leaked to the press a few days after the presentation. Naturally the sponsors were upset by this, but the culprit was never identified. Evidently someone had felt it was in the public interest that this critical report should not be suppressed – and thus turned the function of the study from *improving* to *proving*.

A final example in which evaluation was used to contribute to debates on management training policy was carried out by myself and some colleagues in a major multi-national. Again this was seen largely within the context of *improving*, and semi-structured interviews were conducted with a sample of about thirty managers attending programmes at the company's international management education centre. These interviews looked at the managers' jobs; how the nature and problems of the jobs were changing; and how they felt their training experience was relating, and should relate, to such changes. The report derived from this study also crystallized a number of issues that needed to be considered in future policy formulation. One of these was the need to devise procedures for adapting the training experience to the very different problems and dilemmas faced by the individuals drawn from perhaps a dozen totally different countries. Another product from this study was an attempt to clarify how managers' roles can change and evolve quite significantly over time within their normal work – thus helping to expose problems of 'transfer' into a more dynamic view of the jobs of the managers in the normal work environment.

Management development

At the policy level there is considerable overlap between management development and management training – at least within a single organization. The questions that may be asked are of the same kind, even though they may be slightly different. One frequent question is whether the organization should take responsibility for the career development of all managers, or whether some élite cadre of managers should be given special treatment by being placed on the 'fast track'. Furthermore, if a fast track policy is decided upon, should the associated assessment and career development system be an open one (where all managers are informed about how the organization regards their potential and what they would need to do to improve their management potential); or should it be a closed system, where not only the names of those on the high flier list are kept secret, but also the existence of the system itself is supposed to be kept secret? And indeed, it is quite surprising just how frequently senior managers prefer closed systems and also believe that they are being kept secret.

The above example relates to what might be termed the 'technical' aspects of management development, where it is regarded largely as a separate activity from the mainstream managing of the organization. However, thinking in the USA (largely provoked by attempts to understand why Japanese business is so successful) has regarded management development as being much more closely integrated with the management style and value systems of the organization as a whole. Peters and Waterman (1982) were probably the most prominent voices in this respect, and they placed considerable emphasis upon the development of clearly understood value systems, and the establishment of very supportive climates which try to make most managers and employees feel that they are doing an excellent job.

One implication of this kind of philosophy is that any appraisal systems which are intended to provide feedback on performance to managers and employees should be designed in such a way that most of the information feedback is very positive. Another clear implication is that the main responsibility for building such a climate and ensuring that positive feedback takes place lies entirely with managers from the top to the bottom of the organization – rather than with any personnel or management development specialists. Another influential advocate of this kind of philosophy is Lewis Lehr, chairman of the 3M Company.

He even goes so far as to encourage, and even honour, those who make mistakes within the company – on the grounds that this is the best way of helping managers to take risks and thereby increasing the ability of the organization to learn from its actions. He has but one reservation to this philosophy: 'We expect any mistakes to have originality. We can afford almost any mistake – once.'

So what contribution might evaluation make in this area? Firstly, with regard to the more technical aspects of management development policies there is a role for evaluation in finding out what the effects of those policies are 'on the ground floor'. This is one thing that the management development audit attempts to do in a general way across the whole spectrum of training and development activities. Such evaluative activity could be more concise, for example one might wish to enquire into the effect that the existence of a 'fast track' system has on managers at different stages of their careers. In this case a few careful discussions with selected managers (qualitative interviews), may well suffice. For example, one of the classic problems with such systems was pinpointed by a comment from a middle manager whom I interviewed in one such study a few years ago: 'But you see, the people it really screws up are those like me who just failed to get in.'

This leads to the second main role that evaluation may play in this area which is to stimulate people to ask the right questions about aspects of the organization and the way it treats managers, and to provide some contribution to the debate about those questions. In this case it puts evaluation into the role of offering an interactive dialogue with policy makers, who have responsibility for running the company.

Conclusion

The politics of evaluation at the 'policy' level are largely inescapable, and it is partly in recognition of this that naturalistic approaches have predominated. Where the more traditional experimental research style has been employed (as with MBA programmes in the early 1970s) the results have been either equivocal or negative. And this is not the kind of result that those who sponsor evaluations wish to see.

Interventionalist styles of evaluation have rather less value at the policy level simply because the scale of policy decisions is likely to be beyond the range of most evaluators. And therefore the more illuminative styles seem to have great potential, where they can help to identify and clarify issues that need to be considered when policies are being formulated. When this is combined with the kind of dialogue between managers and specialists suggested in the latter part of this chapter, then there may be much potential for influencing what takes place. And this also brings us a long way from the traditional view of evaluation as a systematic process of feedback and control.

10 Moving on?

Thinking about the purpose and methods of evaluation has progressed considerably in the last twenty or so years; so has evaluation practice. But this progress has been slow – some areas have become quite sophisticated, others have maintained outmoded ideas and practices. There has been, it would seem, little communication and exchange between different schools of evaluation, and between different areas of application. This book has been an attempt to draw together these developments and to examine their application in the management area.

The distinction made between the contexts of education, training and development at various stages in the book has been particularly useful to me in organizing material. But I hope that the adoption of such a wide scope has enabled the range of purposes and styles to be illustrated, and that it has also emphasized how the political aspects of evaluation can vary in different contexts.

There are also a number of 'trends' that have been identified in the book. Some of these trends represent a change in *actual practice* across many organizations and institutions. For example, there does seem to be more acceptance of qualitative data, and slightly less lip service paid to scientific designs. Cost-benefit analysis has quietly slipped off-stage, but no doubt it is still waiting in the wings.

Some of the trends do not represent significant changes in behaviour, but rather seeing or recognizing old things from *new perspectives*. The recognition of organizational pluralities and the different stakeholders to training and development would be one example of this. Another would be the acknowledgement of the political nature of evaluation data, and the fact that many managers' opinions and judgements are not formed in a logical way from valid data carefully presented – but through hunch, intuition and guesswork based on data obtained through natural 'networks'.

A third type of 'trend' may be more a reflection of my own prejudices and beliefs – based, at least, on considerable experience of conducting evaluations in different circumstances. If prejudices they be, then they include a preference for 'interventionalist' styles of evaluation, for collaborative strategies (with co-researchers), and for a greater emphasis on the *learning* potential of evaluation.

I am aware, also, of my views having changed somewhat since the earlier edition of this book was published. This is partly a result of thinking, reading, and discussing evaluation with others, and partly because I have had many more opportunities to test these ideas out in practice; but it is also because outside circumstances have changed. Management education and development continues to change, to evolve, and to develop; therefore the 'job' of evaluation needs to change too. No doubt these circumstances will continue to change, and not necessarily in a linear manner. There will be some movement forwards, and some backwards. Thus it would be unwise to predict the future of evaluation simply as a projection of present trends. But different it will be.

That is why I have not tried to lay down tablets of stone about methods, procedures and philosophies; but to raise issues and to demonstrate some of the complexities inherent in the conduct of evaluation. I hope that what I have to say will not only alert people to a wider range of considerations, but also encourage them to think things out for themselves. And so, I hope, the practice of evaluation will progress. That is why I finish not with a conclusion, but with a question about further progress.

References

Allport, G. W. (1937), *Pattern and Growth in Personality* (republished 1961), Holt, Rinehart and Winston, New York.

Argyris, C. (1980), 'Some Limitations of the Case Method: Experiences in a Management Development Programme', *Academy of Management Review*, Vol. 5, No. 2, pp. 291–8.

Argyris, C., and Schön, D. A. (1974), *Theory in Practice: Increasing Professional Effectiveness*, Josey-Bass, San Francisco.

Armitage, S. (1993), 'Guidelines for Enhancing Learning Opportunities in Computer-based Management Simulations', in D. Saunders (ed.), *Annual Handbook of Simulations and Games*, Kogan Page, London.

Ashton, D. J. L. and Easterby-Smith, M. P. V. (1978), *Management Development in the Organisation*, Macmillan, London.

Bales, R. F. (1950), *Interaction Process Analysis: a Method for the Study of Small Groups*, Addison-Wesley, London.

Bandura, A. (1977), 'Self-Efficacy: Towards a Unifying Theory of Behavioural Change', *Psychological Review*, Vol. 84, Pt. 2, pp. 191–215.

Bannister, D. and Fransella, F. (1971), *Inquiring Man: the Theory of Personal Constructs*, Penguin Books, Harmondsworth.

Becker, H. S. (1979), 'Do Photographs Tell the Truth?', in T. D. Cook and C. S. Reichardt (eds), *Qualitative and Quantitative Methods in Evaluation Research*, Sage, London.

Beckhard, R. and Harris, R. T. (1977), *Organisational Transitions, Managing Complex Change*, Addison-Wesley, London.

Binsted, D. S. and Snell, R. S. (1981), 'The Tutor-Learner Interaction in Management Development. Part I: The Effect of Relationships and

Tutor Facilitating Strategy on Feelings, Learning and Interest', *Personnel Review*, Vol. 10, No. 3, pp. 3–13.

Blake, R. R., Mouton, J. S., Barnes, L. B. and Greiner, L. E. (1964), 'Breakthrough in Organisation Development', *Harvard Business Review*, [November/December].

Bligh, D. (1971), *What's the Use of Lectures?*, Penguin Books, Harmondsworth.

Bloom, B. S. *et al.* (1956), *Taxonomy of Educational Objectives*, David McKay, New York.

Boyatsis, R. E. (1982), *The Competent Manager – A Model for Effective Performance*, Wiley, New York.

Bramley, P. (1991), *Evaluating Training Effectiveness: Translating Theory into Practice*, McGraw-Hill, Maidenhead.

Bray, D. W. (1966), 'Choosing Good Managers', *Foundation for Research on Human Behaviour*, pp. 153–65.

Brewster, C. (1981), 'Evaluation of Management Training: A Focus on Change', in J. Beck and C. Cox (eds), *Advances in Management Education*, Wiley, London.

British Institute of Management (1971), *Business School Programmes: The Requirements of British Manufacturing Industry*, BIM, London, [Owen Report].

Burgoyne, J. G. (1973a), 'An Action Research Experiment in the Evaluation of a Management Development Course', *Journal of Management Studies*, Vol 10, No. 1.

Burgoyne, J. G. (1973b), 'A New Approach to Evaluating Management Development Programmes: Some Exploratory Research', *Personnel Review*, Vol. 2, Autumn, pp. 40–4.

Burgoyne, J. G. (1975), 'The Judgement Process in Management Students' Evaluation of their Learning Experiences', *Human Relations*, Vol. 28, No. 6, pp. 543–69.

Burgoyne, J. G. (1981), 'Planning Management Development Policy', CSML Working Paper, Lancaster University, Lancaster.

Burgoyne, J. G. (1989), 'Creating the Managerial Portfolio: Building on Competency Approaches to Managerial Development', *Management Education and Development*, Vol. 20, Part 1, pp. 56–61.

Burgoyne, J. G. and Singh, R. (1977), 'Evaluation of Training and Education: Micro and Macro Perspectives', *Journal of European Industrial Training*, Vol. 1, No. 1, pp. 17–21.

Burgoyne, J. G. and Hodgson, V. E. (1982), 'An Experiential Approach to Managerial Action', Proceedings of Biennial Conference on Leadership and Managerial Behaviour, Oxford.

Burgoyne, J. G., Boydell, T. H. and Pedler, M. J. (1978), *Self-Development: Theory and Applications, For Practitioners*, ATM, London.

Burgoyne, J. G. and Stuart, R. (1976), 'The Nature, Use and Acquisition of Managerial Skills and Other Attributes', *Personnel Review*, No. 5, PE 4, pp. 19–29.

Buros, O. K. (1978), *Eighth Mental Measurements Yearbook*, The Gryphon Press, University of Nebraska.

Buzan, T. (1974), *Use Your Head*, BBC Publications, London.

Campbell, D. T. and Stanley, J. C. (1966), *Experimental and Quasi-Experimental Design for Research*, Rand McNally, Chicago.

Campbell, J. P., Dunnette, M. D., Lawler, E. E. and Weick, K. E. (1970), *Managerial Behaviour, Performance and Effectiveness*, McGraw Hill, Maidenhead.

Carlson, S. (1951), *Executive Behaviour: A Study of the Work Load and the Working Methods of Managerial Directors*, Strombergs, Stockholm.

Carter, P. and Jackson, N. (1990), 'The Emergence of Postmodern Management?', *Management Education and Development*, Vol. 21, Part 3, pp. 219–28.

Casey, D. (1981), 'Transfer of Learning – There are Two Separate Problems' in J. Beck and C. Cox (eds), *Advances in Management Education*, Wiley, Chichester.

Constable, J. and McCormick, R. (1987), *The Making of British Managers*, British Institute of Management with the Confederation of British Industry, London.

Critten, P. (1982), 'Evaluation as a Process of Revelation'. Paper based on unpublished Ph.D. thesis, presented to conference on Management Education and Development, Lancaster University, Lancaster.

Cronbach, L. J. (1963), 'Course Improvement Through Evaluation', *Teachers College Records*, Vol. 64, pp. 672–83.

Cunliffe, A. (1985), 'Unit Administration in the National Health Service', unpublished M.Phil. thesis, Lancaster University, Lancaster.

Cunningham, I. (1986), *Developing Chief Executives: An Evaluation*, Ashridge Management College, Berkhampstead.

Cyert, R. N. and March, J. G. (1963), *A Behavioural Theory of the Firm*, Prentice-Hall, Englewood Cliffs.

Davies, J. M. and Easterby-Smith, M. P. V. (1984), 'Learning and Developing from Managerial Work Experiences', *Journal of Management Studies*, Vol. 21, Pt. 3, pp. 169–84.

Dearden, G. and Laurillard, D. (1976), 'Progressive Focussing in a Medical School Evaluation'. Paper presented at 2nd Annual Conference of the BERA, London.

Department of Employment (1971), *Glossary of Training Terms*, HMSO, London.

Deutscher, I. (1976), 'Toward Avoiding the Goal-Trap in Evaluation Research' in C. C. Abt (ed.), *The Evaluation of Social Programmes*, p. 249–88, Sage, Beverly Hills.

Douglas, J. D. (1976), *Investigative Social Research: Individual and Team Field Research*, Sage, Beverly Hills.

Easterby-Smith, M. P. V. (1977), 'The Repertory Grid Technique as a Personnel Tool', *Management Decision*, Vol. 14, No. 5, pp. 239–47.

Easterby-Smith, M. P. V. (1979), *Organisational Change and the Individual*. Unpublished Ph.D. thesis, Durham University, Durham.

Easterby-Smith, M. P. V. (1980a), 'The Evaluation of Management Education and Development: an Overview', *Personnel Review*, Vol. 10, Pt. 2, pp. 28–36.

Easterby-Smith, M. P. V. (1980b), 'How to Use Repertory Grid Technique in H.R.D.', *Journal of European Training Monograph*, Vol. 4, No. 2, pp. 1–32.

Easterby-Smith, M. P. V. and Ashton, D. J. L. (1975), 'Using Repertory Grid Technique to Evaluate Management Training', *Personnel Review*, Vol. 4, No. 4, pp. 15–21.

Easterby-Smith, M. P. V. and Davies, J. M. (1983), 'Developing Strategic Thinking', *Long Range Planning*, Vol. 16, No. 4, pp. 39–48.

Easterby-Smith, M. P. V. and Mackness, J. (1992), 'Completing the cycle of evaluation', *Personnel Management* [May].

Easterby-Smith, M. P. V., Krishna, R. and Ashton, D. J. L. (1977), *Design and Make: an Evaluation of an Introductory Programme for Postgraduate Engineers*. Final report to the Training Services Agency, Durham University Business School, Durham.

Easterby-Smith, M. P. V., Braiden, E. M. and Ashton, D J. L. (1980), *Auditing Management Development*, Gower, Aldershot.

Easterby-Smith, M. P. V., Thorpe, R. and Lowe, A. (1991), *Management Research: An Introduction*, Sage, London.

Elden, M. (1981), 'Sharing the Research Work: Participative Research and its Role Demands', in P. Reason and J. Rowan (eds), *Human Inquiry*, Wiley, Chichester.

Eysenck, H. J. and Eysenck, S. B. G. (1967), 'On the Unitary Nature of Extraversion', *Acta Psychologica*, Vol. 26, pp. 383–90.

Fayol, H. (1916), *Administration Industrielle et Générale*, Dunod, Paris.

Fielding, N. G. and Fielding, J. L. (1986), *Linking Data*, Sage, Beverly Hills.

Filstead, W. J. (1979), 'Qualitative Methods: A Needed Perspective in Evaluation Research', in T. D. Cook and C. S. Reichardt (eds), *Qualitative and Quantitative Methods in Evaluation Research*, Sage, Beverly Hills.

French, W. L. and Bell, C. H. (1978), *Organisation Development: Behavioural Science Interventions for Organisation Improvement*, Prentice-Hall, New Jersey.

Gibb, A. A. (1977), 'An Investment Appraisal of Training', *Journal of European Training*, Vol. 1, Pt. 1, pp. 19–33.

Gibson, M. (1983), 'Formative Evaluation: The Effect of Group Development', *Management Education and Development*, Vol. 14, Pt. 3, pp. 153–7.

Glaser, D. G. and Strauss, A. L. (1967), *The Discovery of Grounded Theory: Strategies for Qualitative Research*, Aldine, New York.

Guba, E. G. and Lincoln, Y. S. (1989), *Fourth Generation Evaluation*, Sage, London.

Graduate Management Admissions Council (1990), *Leadership in a Chang-*

ing World: The Future Role of Management Education, GMAC, Los Angeles.

Gulick, L. H. (1937), 'Notes on the Theory of Organisation', in L. H. Gulick and L. F. Urwick (eds), *Papers on the Science of Administration*, Columbia University, New York.

Hamblin, A. C. (1968), 'Training in Evaluation: A Discussion of Some Problems', in R. J. Hacon (ed.), *Organisational Necessities and Individual Needs*, ATM Occasional Paper, No. 5, pp. 70–81, Blackwell, Oxford.

Hamblin, A. C. (1974), *Evaluation and Control of Training*, McGraw-Hill, Maidenhead.

Hamilton, D. (1976), *Curriculum Evaluation*, Open Books, Shepton Mallet.

Handy, C. B. (1976), *Understanding Organisations*, Penguin Books, Harmondsworth.

Handy, C. B., Gow, I., Gordon, C., Randlesome, C. and Moloney, M. (1987), *The Making of Managers*, National Economic Development Council with the British Institute of Management and the Manpower Services Commission, London.

Hayes, R. H. and Abernathy, W. J. (1980), 'Managing our Way to Economic Decline', *Harvard Business Review*, Vol. 58, Pt. 8, pp. 67–77.

Hayes, C., Fonda, N., Pope, M., Stuart, R. and Townsend, K. (1983), *Training for Skill Ownership: Learning to Take it With You*, Institute of Manpower Studies, Brighton.

Herzberg, F., Mausner, B. and Snyderman, B. B. (1959), *The Motivation to Work*, Wiley, New York.

Hesseling, P. (1966), *Strategy of Evaluation Research in the Field of Supervisory and Management Training*, Van Gorcum, Anssen.

Hodgson, V. E. and Reynolds, P. M. (1981), 'The Hidden Experience of Learning Events – Illusions of Involvement', *Personnel Review*, Vol. 10, No. 1, pp. 26–9.

Hofstede, G. (1980), *Cultures' Consequences*, Sage, London.

Hogarth, R. M. (1979), *Evaluating Management Education*, Wiley, Chichester.

Honey, P. and Mumford, A. (1982), *A Manual of Learning Styles*. Privately published.

Hopwood, A. (1979), 'Criteria for Corporate Effectiveness', in M. Brodie and R. Bennett (eds), *Managerial Effectiveness*, Thames Valley Regional Management Centre, Slough.

Jameson, J. M. (1980), 'Evaluation: H.C.I.T.B. Small Business Programme'. Unpublished dissertation for Diploma in Management Learning, Lancaster University, Lancaster.

Jenkins, D., Simmons, H. and Walker, R. (1981), ' "Thou Nature art my Goddess". Naturalistic Enquiry in Educational Evaluation', *Cambridge Journal of Education*, Vol. 11, No. 3, pp. 169–89.

Jones, J. H. G. and Moxham, J. (1969), 'Costing the Benefits of Training', *Personnel Management*, Vol. 1, Pt. 4, pp. 22–8.

Kelly, G. A. (1955), *The Psychology of Personal Constructs*, Norton, New York.

Kirkpatrick, D. L. (1959/60), 'Techniques for evaluating training programs: Parts 1 to 4', *Journal of the American Society for Training and Development* [November, December, January, February].

Kirkpatrick, D. L. (1967), 'Evaluation of Training', in R. L. Craig and L. R. Bittel (eds), *Training and Development Handbook*, ASTD, McGraw-Hill, New York.

Kolb, D. H. and Fry, R. (1975), 'Towards an Applied Theory of Experiential Learning', in C. L. Cooper (ed.), *Theories of Group Process*, Wiley, New York.

Kolb, D. A., Rubin, I. M. and McIntyre, J. (1971), *Organisational Psychology*, Prentice-Hall, Englewood Cliffs.

Kotter, J. P. and Lawrence, P. (1974), *Mayors in Action: Five Studies in Urban Governance*, Wiley, New York.

Krech, D., Crutchfield, R. S. and Ballachey, E. L. (1962), *Individual in Society*, McGraw-Hill, New York.

Kuhn, T. S. (1962), *The Structure of Scientific Revolutions*, University of Chicago Press, Chicago.

Lawrence, P. (1992), 'Management Development in Europe: A Study in Cultural Contrasts', *Human Resource Management Journal*, Vol. 3, No. 1, pp. 11–23.

Livingston, J. S. (1971), 'The Myth of the Well-Educated Manager', *Harvard Business Review*, Vol. 49, pp. 79–89.

Lock, A. (1992), Personal communication to the author.

MacDonald-Ross, M. (1973), 'Behavioural Objectives: A Critical Review', *Instructional Science*, Vol. 2, pp. 1–52.

Mant, A. (1969), *The Experienced Manager – A Major Resource*, BIM, London.

Marsh, J. (1983), 'The Boredom of Study: A Study of Boredom', *Management Education and Development*, Vol. 14, Pt. 2, pp. 120–35.

Massarik, F. (1981), 'The Interviewing Process Reexamined', in P. Reason and J. Rowan, *Human Inquiry*, Wiley, Chichester.

Mayo, E. (1946), *Human Problems of an Industrial Civilisation*, Macmillan, London.

Megginson, D. and Pedler, M. (1975), 'Developing Structures and Technology for the Learning Community', *Journal of European Training*, Vol. 5, No. 5, pp. 262–75.

Mintzberg, H. (1973), *The Nature of Managerial Work*, Harper and Row, New York.

Mintzberg, H. (1976), 'Planning on the Left Side and Managing on the Right', *Harvard Business Review*, Vol. 54 [July-August] pp. 49–58.

Newby, A. C. (1992), *Training Evaluation Handbook*, Gower, Aldershot.

Nunally, J. C. (1967), *Psychometric Theory*, McGraw-Hill, New York.

Oppenheim, A. N. (1966), *Questionnaire Design and Attitude Measurement*, Heinemann, London.

Parlett, M. and Hamilton, D. (1972), 'Evaluation as Illumination: A New

Approach to the Study of Innovatory Programmes', *Occasional Paper 9*, Centre for Research in Educational Sciences, University of Edinburgh, Edinburgh.

Parlett, M. and Dearden, G. (1981), *Introduction to Illuminative Evaluation*, Society for Research into Higher Education, Guildford.

Partridge, S. E. and Scully, D. (1979), 'Cases Versus Gaming', *Management Education and Development*, Vol. 10, Pt. 3, pp. 172–80.

Pask, G. and Scott, B. C. E. (1972), 'Learning Strategies and Individual Competence', *International Journal of Man-Machine Studies*, Vol. 4, pp. 217–53.

Patton, M. Q. (1978), *Utilization-Focussed Evaluation*, Sage, Beverly Hills.

Patton, M. Q. (1980), *Qualitative Evaluation Methods*, Sage, Beverly Hills.

Patton, M. Q. (1981), *Creative Evaluation*, Sage, Beverly Hills.

Peat, Marwick, Mitchell and Company (1979), 'An Approach to Costing Training: A Feasibility Study', *Report to the Manpower Services Commission*, Training Services Division, London.

Perrow, C. (1971), *Organisational Analysis: A Sociological View*, Tavistock Publications, London.

Peters, T. J. and Waterman, R. H. (1982), *In Search of Excellence*, Harper and Row, New York.

Pettigrew, A. M. (1973), *The Politics of Organisational Decision-Making*, Tavistock Publications, London.

Phillips, J. J. (1987), *Handbook of Training Evaluation and Measurement Methods*, Gulf, Houston.

Porter, L. W. and McKibbin, L. E. (1988), *Management Education and Development: Drift or Thrust into the 21st Century?*, McGraw-Hill, New York.

Punch, M. (1986), *The Politics and Ethics of Fieldwork*, Sage, Beverly Hills.

Pym, D. L. A. (1968), 'Organisation Evaluation and Management Training', *Journal of Management Studies*, Vol. 5, Pt. 2, pp. 167–83.

Rackham, N. (1973), 'Recent Thoughts on Evaluation', *Industrial and Commercial Training*, Vol. 5, No. 10, pp. 454–61.

Rackham, J. J. and Reynolds, P. M. (1971), 'Experiment in Management Studies', *Management Education and Development*, Vol. 1, Pt. 3, pp. 124–36.

Rackham, N., Honey, P. and Colbert, M. (1971), *Developing Interactive Skills*, Wellens, Northampton.

Reason, P. and Rowan J. (eds) (1981), *Human Inquiry: A Sourcebook of New Paradigm Research*, Wiley, Chichester.

Reichardt, C. S. and Cook, T. D. (1979), 'Beyond Qualitative *versus* Quantitative Methods', in T. D. Cook and C. S. Reichardt (eds), *Qualitative and Quantitative Methods in Evaluation Research*, Sage, Beverly Hills.

Revans, R. W. (1971), *Developing Effective Managers*, Praeger, New York.

Reynolds, P. M. (1979), 'Experiential Learning: A Declining Force for Change', *Management Education and Development*, Vol. 10, Pt. 2, pp. 89–99.

Reynolds, P. M. and Hodgson, V. E. (1980), 'Participants' Experiences as a Basis for Course Improvement', *Management Education and Development*, Vol. 11, Pt. 3, pp. 210–18.

Rogers, A., Cooper, C. L. and Burgoyne, J. G. (1977), 'Evaluation of Management Education: The State of the Art', in D. Ashton (ed.), *Management Bibliographies and Reviews*, Vol. 3, MCB, Bradford.

Rossi, P. H., Freeman, H. E. and Wright, S. R. (1979), *Evaluation: A Systematic Approach*, Sage, Beverly Hills.

Ruddock, R. (1981), *Evaluation: A Consideration of Principles and Methods*, Manchester Monographs 18.

Ryle, G. (1949), *The Concept of Mind*, Penguin Books, Harmondsworth.

Salinger, R. D. and Deming, B. S. (1982), 'Practical Strategies for Evaluating Training', *Training and Development Journal*, Vol. 36, No. 8, pp. 20–9.

Scriven, M. (1967), 'The Methodology of Evaluation', in R. W. Tyler, R. M. Gagne and M. Scriven (eds), *Perspectives of Curriculum Evaluation*, AERA Monograph Series on Curriculum Evaluation No. 1, Rand-McNally, Chicago.

Scriven, M. (1972), 'Pros and Cons about Goal-Free Evaluation', *Evaluation Comment*, Vol. 3, No. 4, pp. 1–4.

Scriven, M. (1974), 'Evaluation Perspectives and Procedures', in W. J. Popham, *Evaluation in Education*, McCuthlan Corporation, California.

Schein, E. (1970), *Organisational Psychology*, Prentice-Hall, Englewood Cliffs.

Siegel, S. (1956), *Nonparametric Statistics for the Behavioural Sciences*, McGraw-Hill, New York.

Simon, H. A. (1959), *Administrative Behaviour*, 2nd edition, Macmillan, London.

Snyder, B. R. (1971), *The Hidden Curriculum*, Knopf, New York.

Stake, R. E. (1980), 'Responsive Evaluation', Mimeograph, University of Illinois.

Stewart, R. (1967), *Managers and their Jobs*, Macmillan, London.

Stewart, R. (1976), *Contrasts in Management: A Study of the Different Types of Managers' Jobs: Their Demands and Choices*, McGraw-Hill, Maidenhead.

Stewart, R. (1982), *Choices for the Manager: A Guide to Managerial Work and Behaviour*, McGraw-Hill, Maidenhead.

Stewart, V. and Stewart, A. (1978), *Managing the Manager's Growth*, Gower, Aldershot.

Stewart, A. and Stewart, V. (1981a), *Tomorrow's Managers Today: The Identification and Development of Management Potential*, Institute of Personnel Management, London.

Stewart, V. and Stewart, A. (1981b), *Business Applications of Repertory Grid*, McGraw-Hill, Maidenhead.

Sturrock, J. (ed.) (1979), *Structuralism and Since: From Lévy Strauss to Derrida*, Oxford Paperbacks, Oxford.

Thorpe, R. and Best, A. (1989), *A Study into Early Learning of Participants in Employment Training in the South Yorkshire Area*, Manchester Polytechnic.

Thurley, K. E. and Wirdenius, H. (1973), *Supervision: A Reappraisal*, Heinemann, London.

Thurley, K. E., Graves, D. and Hult, M. (no date), *An Evaluation Strategy for Management Development*. Unpublished report.

Torbert, W. R. (1981), 'Why Educational Research has been so Uneducational: The Case for a New Model of Social Science based on Collaborative Enquiry', in P. Reason and J. Rowan, *Human Inquiry*, Wiley, Chichester.

Warr, P. B., Bird, M. W. and Rackham, N. (1970), *Evaluation of Management Training*, Gower, Aldershot.

Webb, E., Campbell, D., Schwartz, R. and Sechrest, L. (1967), *Unobtrusive Measures: Non-Reactive Research in the Social Sciences*, Rand McNally, Chicago.

Whitley, R., Thomas, A. and Marceau, J. (1981), *Masters of Business? Business Schools and Business Graduates in Britain and France*, Tavistock Publications, London.

Wilson, J. (1970), 'The BIM Course Assessment Service', *Management Education and Development*, Vol. 1, Pt. 2, pp. 72–7.

Index

Building a Better Team
A handbook for
managers and facilitators

Peter Moxon

Team leadership and team development are central to the modern manager's ability to "achieve results through other people". Successful team building requires knowledge and skill, and the aim of this handbook is to provide both. Using a unique blend of concepts, practical guidance and exercises, the author explains both the why and the how of team development.

Drawing on his extensive experience as manager and consultant, Peter Moxon describes how groups develop, how trust and openness can be encouraged, and the likely problems overcome. As well as detailed advice on the planning and running of teambuilding programmes the book contains a series of activities, each one including all necessary instructions and support material.

Irrespective of the size or type of organization involved, <u>Building a Better Team</u> offers a practical, comprehensive guide to managers, facilitators and team leaders seeking improved performance.

Contents
Introduction • Part I: Teams and Teambuilding • Introduction • Teams and team effectiveness • Teambuilding • Summary • Part II: Designing and Running Teambuilding Programmes • Introduction • Diagnosis • Design and planning • Running the session • Follow-up • Part III: Teambuilding Tools and Techniques • Introduction • Diagnosis exercise • Getting started exercises • Improving team effectiveness exercises • Index.

1993   250 pages   0 566 07424 9

Gower

Choosing and Using Training Consultants

Diane Bailey and Clare Sproston

As the need for training continues to grow, many organizations are finding that they can no longer fulfil all the demands for training from their own resources. More and more therefore they are turning to specialist consultants for help. Personnel and training managers and others involved are having to develop the skills of working with consultants, many of whom are themselves new to the business.

The present book has been produced to answer precisely two key questions: How to choose a consultant and how to ensure the maximum benefit to the organization. It is based on the authors' own experience of working as consultants with a wide variety of clients. They provide a step-by-step guide designed to achieve a relationship that is as productive as possible. Among the topics covered are:

- preparing the ground
- finding and selecting a consultant
- preparing a brief
- considering the proposal
- contracting
- managing the project
- managing the consultant
- evaluating results

The book also functions as working document. By completing the instruments, charts and activities it contains the reader can develop a personal reference and action manual. For anyone contemplating the use of consultants for training this book is the most helpful starting point imaginable.

1993   120 pages   0 566 07328 5

Gower

Guide to In-Company Training Methods

Leslie Rae

Learning at the workplace is usually the cheapest way to train - it is often the best. Leslie Rae's latest book covers the processes and the skills involved in training without incurring the expense of sending people on external courses. The methods he describes range from "sitting next to Nellie" through delegation, coaching, mentoring, team development and self-development to one-to-one instruction. He explains in detail the structures and techniques required and provides checklists, formats and guidelines to supplement the text.

Both line managers and professional trainers will profit from a study of this important new book by one of the UK's best known training experts.

Contents

Why in-company training? • People and learning • Options in training • The skills of the trainer • GAFO and mentoring • Delegation •Coaching • The structure of coaching • One-to-one instruction - the initial stages • One-to-one instruction - stages, design and packages • One-to-one instruction - detailed preparation • Producing and using instructional aids - the simpler aids • Producing and using instructional aids - other aids • One-to-one instruction - the remaining stages • Other in-company training methods • Appendix: Summary checklist for in-company training • References and recommended reading • Index.

1992   190 pages   0 566 072971

Gower

Handbook of
Management Games
Fifth Edition
Chris Elgood

What kinds of management game are now available? How do they differ from one another? How do they compare with other ways of learning? Where can I find the most suitable games for the objectives I have in mind? <u>Handbook of Management Games</u> offers detailed answers to these questions and many others. For this fifth edition the text has been virtually rewritten to take account of new developments. The result is a comprehensive and up-to-date guide to choosing and using games for management training and development.

Part One of the Handbook examines the characteristics and applications of the different types of game. It explains the methods by which they promote learning and the situations for which they are best suited.

Part Two comprises a directory of some 300 management games, compiled from questionnaires completed by their producers. Each game is described in terms of its target group, subject areas, nature and purpose, and the means by which the outcome is established and made known. The entries also give administrative details such as the number of players, the number of teams and the time required. A specially designed system of indexes enables readers to locate precisely those games that would be suitable for their own situation.

In its new edition Chris Elgood's Handbook remains an indispensable work for anyone concerned with management development.

1993   352 pages   0 566 07306 4

Gower

How Managers Can Develop Managers

Alan Mumford

Managers are constantly being told that they are responsible for developing other managers. This challenging book explains why and how this should be done.

Moving beyond the familiar territory of appraisal, coaching and courses, Professor Mumford examines ways of using day-to-day contact to develop managers. The emphasis is on learning from experience - from the job itself, from problems and opportunities, from bosses, mentors and colleagues.

Among the topics covered are:
- recognizing learning opportunities
- understanding the learning process
- what being helped involves
- the skills required to develop others
- the idea of reciprocity ("I help you, you help me")

Throughout the text there are exercises designed to connect the reader's own experience to the author's ideas. The result is a powerful and innovative work from one of Europe's foremost writers on management development.

Contents

1993   200 pages   0 566 07403 6

Gower

How to Write a Training Manual

John Davis

In association with the Institute of Training and Development

Course documentation is a subject largely ignored in trainer education. Yet it is central to success in the training room. A well-thought-out training manual:

- ensures high-quality presentation first time and every time a course is run

- promotes better course management and more professional delivery

- facilitates the review and, where necessary, the modification of training material

- leads to the correct balance between creativity, flexibility and professional discipline

John Davis' new book - the first of its kind - shows how to prepare documentation using a format designed to clarify content, timing, delivery, pace and style. Drawing on his own extensive experience, he offers practical guidelines supported throughout by detailed examples. For trainers and training managers seeking to improve their performance, his advice is not to be missed.

1992   152 pages   0 566 07325 0

Gower

Problem Solving in Groups

Second Edition

Mike Robson

Modern scientific research has demonstrated that groups are likely to solve problems more effectively than individuals. As most of us knew already, two heads (or more) are better than one. In organizations it makes sense to harness the power of the group both to deal with problems already identified and to generate ideas for enhancing effectiveness by reducing costs, increasing productivity and the like.

In this revised and updated edition of his successful book, Mike Robson first introduces the concepts and methods involved. Then, after setting out the advantages of the group approach, he examines in detail each of the eight key problem solving techniques. The final part of the book explains how to present proposed solutions, how to evaluate results and how to ensure that the group process runs smoothly.

With its practical tone, its down-to-earth style and lively visuals, this is a book that will appeal strongly to managers and trainers looking for ways of improving their organization's and their department's performance.

Contents

1993   176 pages   0 566 07414 1 Hardback   0 566 07415 X Paperback

Gower

Running an Effective Training Session

Patrick Forsyth
of
Touchstone Training and Consultancy

This down-to-earth guide to planning and delivering a training session will be welcomed by new and experienced trainers alike - as well as by line managers and other professionals with training responsibility. In his latest book Patrick Forsyth takes the reader step- by-step through the process of structuring the session and preparing materials, before covering the presentational techniques involved in detail. The final section is concerned with following up in terms of evaluation and establishing links to further training . The user-friendly text is supported throughout by examples.

For anyone involved in training, Patrick Forsyth's new book represents a painless way to improve performance.

Contents

Introduction • Establishing a basis • Planning the session • Preparing course materials • Running the session: presentational techniques • Running the session: participative techniques • Following up • Appendix: ready-to-use training material • Index

1992   142 pages   0 566 07320 X

Gower

Training Evaluation Handbook

A C Newby

Based on the author's highly successful <u>Training Evaluation Audit Method (TEAM)</u> this new book will help trainers in any kind of organization to develop more effective programmes. The first part of the book examines the strategic role of training evaluation and discusses some of the political issues involved. Part II presents a range of techniques for improving training effectiveness, and shows how to develop instruments that both assess and reinforce learning. In the final part a series of case studies shows how the author's methods have been used in a wide variety of businesses and functions. If what you are looking for is a systematic way of reviewing and strengthening the training provision in your own organization, then <u>Training Evaluation Handbook</u> is for you.

Contents

1992   324 pages   0 566 02837 9

Gower

35 Checklists for Human Resource Management

Ian MacKay

*In association with the Institute of
Training and Development*

The late Ian MacKay started producing his checklists in the early years of
his work as a lecturer in human resource management. They reflected his
view that the role of the lecturer is not so much to teach as to help others
to learn and, above all, to think for themselves.

From 1985 onwards, Ian MacKay's checklists were a regular - and out-
standingly popular - feature of the Institute of Training and Development's journal. A collection in book form, 35 Checklists for Human
Resource Development, was published in 1989 and has found an apprecia-
tive, and steadily growing, readership. This companion volume covers a
wide variety of human resource issues, from apparently mundane tasks
like designing application forms to issues of the utmost sensitivity like
appraisal, grievance-handling and redundancy policy.

As in the previous volume, the checklists are not designed to provide easy
answers. What they will do is help you to think in a structured way about
your attitudes and behaviour. Your responses can then become a basis for
increasing your effectiveness.

Personnel specialists, and others involved in human resource management,
will find working through the checklists a challenging and rewarding
exercise.

1993   184 pages   0 566 07433 8

Gower